The Bollywood Pocketbook of Iconic Places

Diptakirti Chaudhuri is a marketer by day and a writer by night. He is passionate about and writes on Hindi cinema. He has written six books including three on Bollywood trivia, one on the history of Bollywood and one on legendary screenwriters Salim–Javed. He divides his time between his family in Bangalore and his work in Pune. Outside of real life, he can be found at his blog (diptakirti.com) and on Twitter (@diptakirti).

The Bollywood Pocketbook of Iconic Places

Diptakirti Chaudhuri

First published in 2022 by Hachette India
(Registered name: Hachette Book Publishing India Pvt. Ltd)
An Hachette UK company
www.hachetteindia.com

1

ISBN 978-93-91028-35-0

Hachette Book Publishing India Pvt. Ltd
4th & 5th Floors, Corporate Centre,
Plot No. 94, Sector 44, Gurugram – 122003, India

Typeset in Arno Pro 11/16
Typeset by InoSoft Systems, Noida

Printed and bound in India by
Manipal Technologies Limited, Manipal

To Pishimoni

'Yehi woh jagah hai, yehi woh fizayein,
yehi par kabhi aap humse miley thay…'

– From Brij's *Yeh Raat Phir Na Aayegi*
(written by S.H. Bihari)

Contents

Watson's Hotel

Bombay, 1896

'India did not wait for morning, it began at the hotel — straight away. The lobbies and halls were full of turbaned, and fez'd, and embroidered, cap'd, and barefooted, and cotton-clad dark natives…in the dining-room every man's own private native servant standing behind his chair, and dressed for a part in the Arabian Nights,' wrote Mark Twain on his visit to Bombay (now Mumbai) in January 1896, while '*Following the Equator*' – the title of his resultant book. The hotel he was referring to was Watson's Hotel, then Bombay's finest hospitality establishment, and his sense of wonder is palpable in his writing. He came to Watson's six months before it became the exact location where India's cinematic journey started.

The first exhibition of cinema happened in Paris – on 28 December 1895 – by the Lumière brothers, where 10 short films were screened in a hall called Salon Indien. Less than seven months later, cinema had arrived at Bombay, India – Watson's Hotel, to be precise – to show the moving pictures, organized by Marius Sestier (an agent of the Lumière Brothers). Bombay's leading newspapers, *The Times of India* and *Bombay Gazette*, carried ads for the spectacle – 'The marvel of the century… the wonder of the world… Living photographic pictures in life-size reproductions' – on the morning of the show, 7 July 1896. Six films, each about a minute long, were shown and Bombay's well-heeled watched it for the princely sum of Re. 1 per ticket. Shows ran for three more days at Watson's before shifting to a much larger venue, the 1,400-seater Novelty Theatre, at tickets ranging from eight annas (half a rupee) to ₹2. While the exact numbers of people in attendance are not available, articles describing the experience appeared in all kinds of newspapers – English, Gujarati and Marathi. The cinema bug had truly bitten the Indian population, and shows soon spread all over the country, in cities like Calcutta (now Kolkata) and Madras (now Chennai). Novelty Theatre continued to regularly run cinema shows after this.

The first venue for cinema in India – Watson's Hotel – had

more to its name beyond introducing the Indian populace to cinema. It was constructed entirely of cast-iron, the frames were made in England, shipped to India and assembled here. A much-admired piece of architecture, it was an 'Europeans Only' hotel, and an urban legend goes that Jamsetji Tata was refused entry into Watson's. That's when he decided to build a grander hotel (the Taj Mahal Palace Hotel, as we know it now) in response. While this is probably not true, the emergence of the new hotel, along with owner John Watson's death, rubbed away its sheen. By 1920, it was no longer a hotel, and right now, it is a rather precarious structure – called Esplanade Mansion – housing small offices and cubicles. The place which introduced India to cinema is now on its last legs.

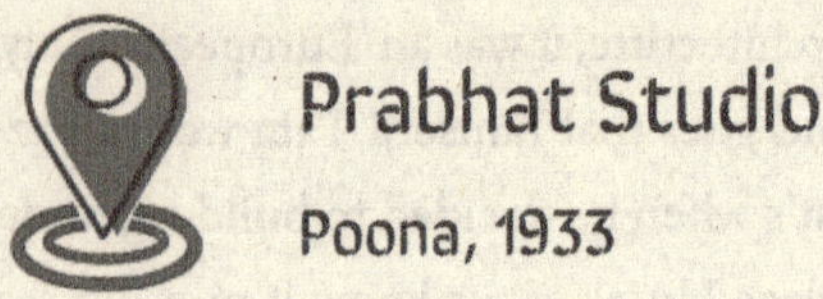

Before Bombay became the nerve-centre of Hindi cinema, there were three nodes in India's fledgling movie industry. The Big Three of pre-Independence Indian cinema were The Bombay Talkies (Bombay), New Theatres (Calcutta) and Prabhat Film Company (Poona). The last two had bilingual output, and held their own for more than a quarter of a century.

Prabhat Film Company was started in Kolhapur by V.G. Damle, S. Fatelal, V. Shantaram, K. Dhaibar and S. Kulkarni – the first three having cut their film-making teeth with Baburao Painter, another pioneering figure in Indian cinema. They moved to Pune in 1933 and opened Prabhat Studio in a 28-acre plot that would eventually become a landmark in the city. Prabhat had an impressive roster of films – including *Ayodhyecha Raja* (the first talkie in Marathi), *Sant Tukaram* (a massive critical and commercial success that was awarded at the Venice Film Festival in 1937) and *Duniya Na Mane* (a bilingual social commentary with far-reaching impact) – but progressive themes were only a part of their reputation. They had a very competent art department, creating some of the finest sets of the times – using high-quality plaster and draperies. It was also a place where women from respectable families could come to work, at a time when cinema was considered a disreputable profession. Actresses like Durga Khote and Shanta Apte[1] got their first breaks at Prabhat Studio, as did Guru Dutt (from 1944–1947), who worked as an actor, assistant director and choreographer. This was the place he developed a lifelong friendship with Dev Anand, who also got his first break at Prabhat. Unfortunately, Dutt and Anand found success when the studio was in a decline – after V. Shantaram had left in early 1942 and Damle had passed away

1. In 1939, Shanta Apte went on a hunger strike at the gates of Prabhat Studio, protesting the company's decision to withhold her salary for a few days of absence. She, like all actors and technicians of the time, was hired on a salary and bound by a contract. Apte's hunger strike – unique in the annals of Indian cinema – was her way of highlighting that she was underworked and underpaid by the company.

in 1945. With actors and technicians preferring to work for a fee per film, instead of a monthly salary, the studio system itself was seeing the end of the road. The company somehow continued till it was liquidated in 1953, but the location – Prabhat Studio – was destined for even greater things.

When the Film and Television Institute of India (FTII) started in 1961, it sprung up in the same location – using the old studio floors, forest-like ambience and tree-lined avenues to great effect. The space that the studio had, to accommodate guests who came to watch the shooting, now gave students the creative expanse to become world-class artistes. Historical artefacts from the Prabhat Studio era – projectors, lamps, film cans – are still found in the premises, and the farthest corner of the campus still has a Shantaram Pond, named after the legendary director.

FTII is that one physical location on which an overwhelming majority of India's finest cinematic talent has set foot, as students and faculty. That it is located in one of the country's oldest studios shows us just how the past of Indian cinema is still shaping the future of the art form.

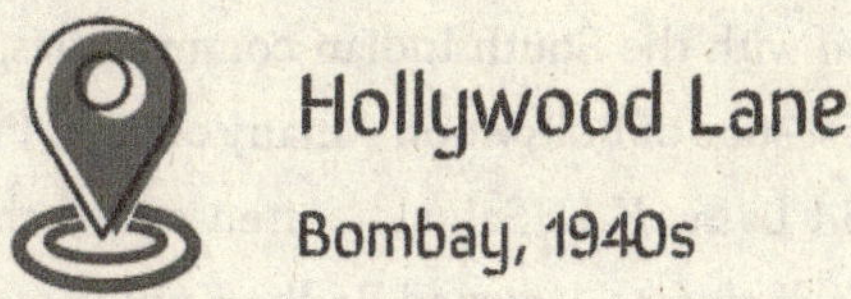

Hollywood Lane

Bombay, 1940s

Imagine a place where K.L. Saigal organizes mehfils and film screenings on a building's terrace. Imagine Prithviraj Kapoor donning the role of night watchman in real life, when communal riots spread through the city, his baritone alerting everyone at regular intervals. Imagine Prithviraj's son, Raj, organizing plays for the neighbourhood – even charging a small price for entry. For a while, in the 1940s, all of this happened on Matunga's R.P. Masani Road – also called Punjabi Galli – but known as Hollywood Lane, thanks to its celebrity residents.

Matunga (along with Dadar) was the city's first planned suburb, and was created by Bombay Improvement Trust in the early twentieth century to house a new professional class, especially from South India. To keep enough space for civic amenities while accommodating the booming population, multi-storied apartment blocks started coming up. But before Matunga became associated with the South Indian communities, it was home to the earliest stars of Bollywood – many of them Punjabi.

On Hollywood Lane, K.L. Saigal – often called the first singing star of Hindi cinema – owned Radha Kunj (now Amar Kunj), a bungalow that since houses the Saigal Memorial Trust. Thanks to the singer's legendary status, the bungalow saw several visitors like Lata Mangeshkar and Bal Thackeray – both of whom were then ascending the stairs of stardom. One of Saigal's tenants was the character actor Madan Puri (whose younger brother, Amrish, also stayed with him for a while).

The star power of the road went up significantly when Prithviraj Kapoor moved to Bombay from Calcutta in 1939, and took up residence here. He not only moved in with his clan, but his home often served as a refuge for young men who had come to Bombay to try their luck in cinema (not to mention, the helping hands of Prithvi Theatres). Soon, school friends of the neighbours' kids would drop in on some pretext, but really to get a glimpse of the dashing Shashi Kapoor.

And beyond these two luminaries, Hollywood Lane derived its name from a host of other film industry denizens. Character actor Manmohan Krishna (who was also a professor of physics) used to tutor some of the kids living there in maths. The suave villain K.N. Singh, character actor Jayant (incidentally, Amjad Khan's father), actor and eventual Dadasaheb Phalke awardee P. Jairaj[2], legendary singer Manna Dey, music director Anil Biswas and Kathak dancer Sitara Devi all lived on Hollywood Lane at different points in time. If we allow tangential residents, actress Vidya Sinha's uncle lived nearby and Mithun Chakraborty also lived here for a short while.

The mid-1950s saw an exodus of film folks from all parts of Bombay towards the newly forming suburbs of Juhu and Bandra (Pali Hill). Their growing stature and the cheaper real estate rates there meant they could build more spacious, luxurious bungalows. The legends of Hollywood Lane also moved out one by one, and the sun slowly set on this boulevard.

2. Hollywood Lane can boast of at least five residents – Prithviraj Kapoor, Raj Kapoor, Shashi Kapoor, P. Jairaj and Manna Dey – who had received Indian cinema's highest award. (Pali Hill is likely to be the only other area with more!)

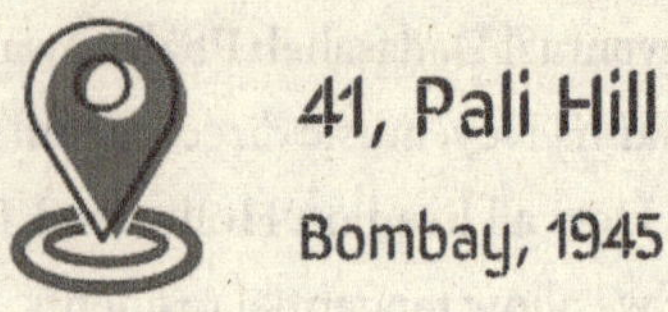

41, Pali Hill

Bombay, 1945

Chetan Anand had come to Bombay on the promise of a film role, that too at a fat salary. The film flopped, the salary stopped and he was no longer in the running to become an actor. His younger brother, Dev, had also come to Bombay, and had found a job at the censor office of the Indian postal department. Chetan could only afford to rent a dilapidated bungalow in a distant location called Bandra, which was not even considered a part of Bombay then. Real estate aficionados of Mumbai would sigh at the rent (₹ 50 per month) and the location (Pali Hill).

Over the next few years, 41, Pali Hill became a buzzing hub of cultural activity – it started as a theatre group, but attracted musicians, singers, dancers, writers and artists, apart from actors. The three Anand brothers – Chetan, Dev and 11-year old Vijay – were at the centre of it. Their journey in cinema and their eventual production house – Navketan Films – germinated from this 'arthouse'.

The entire group at 41, Pali Hill were talented youngsters, all of them taking baby steps into the world of cinema and the arts. Zohra Sehgal, then a gifted dancer, was a regular presence at the house, as were legendary classical musicians, Ali Akbar Khan and Ravi Shankar. They ended up composing the music either for Navketan Films (*Aandhiyan* and *Humsafar* by Ali Akbar Khan) or for Chetan Anand's directorial ventures (*Neecha Nagar* by Ravi Shankar). Writer–director Khwaja Ahmad Abbas was also often found at the bungalow, as were Raj Khosla and Sachin Dev Burman (who had decided not to return to Calcutta after being offered a film by the Anands).

Abbas wrote a play, *Zubeida,* which was performed by the group under the direction of Balraj Sahni, who had also gravitated towards this group after his stint in London. Chetan was cast in the lead role, while Dev was the second lead. Ironically, Sahni got exasperated with Dev's acting skills (or the lack of it), and told the youngster, 'Take it from me, you will never become an actor.' The play flopped, but the acting bug had bitten Dev and he soon left his cushy government job to work at Poona's (now Pune) Prabhat Studios.

The congregation at 41, Pali Hill didn't last a very long time. People had their differences, they built their own partnerships, and their struggles – successful or otherwise – pulled them apart. But it remains a symbol of artistic energy, where a bunch of youngsters with raw talent and liberal views came together to work in a highly creative environment. When Dev Anand became a star, he chose to buy a bungalow almost next door, and lived there for three decades.[3] Initially, his bungalow, then his penthouse atop a multi-storied building, as well as his recording studio, stood at nearly the adjacent plot. He had named his bungalow 'Anand'.

3. Guru Dutt also bought land and built a majestic bungalow at 48, Pali Hill, which he eventually demolished after his wife Geeta Dutt developed an aversion for it.

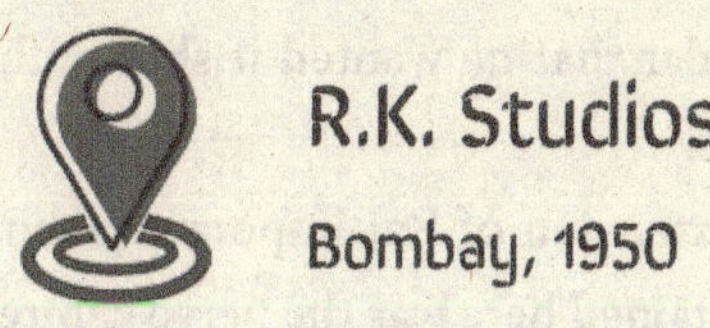

R.K. Studios

Bombay, 1950

'The gates to a timeless legacy will soon open to tell your story,' the advertisement said, talking about a luxury apartment complex made in the Bombay Art Deco style. This proclamation wouldn't have got a second glance from most, unless you saw the name of the property. Godrej RKS is being built on land once owned by India's greatest showman and home to Hindi cinema's first family.

When Raj Kapoor produced his first film (*Aag*) at the age of 24, he was called India's youngest producer. The journey of R.K. Films started then, but the studio itself came two years later – inaugurated on Dussehra of 1950 in a bit of a hurry. The opening sequence to be shot at the studio set the tone for the great things to come. *Awara*'s iconic dream sequence (with the finale '*Ghar aaya mera pardesi*' song) was shot in an incomplete studio – which didn't even have a roof at that time – because Raj Kapoor was particular that he wanted it shot within the premises of R.K. Studios.

The studio was an extension of Raj Kapoor's personality, and the cottage he maintained here was the nerve centre of his creativity. This house hosted co-stars, musicians, writers, friends and colleagues, and was the venue of hundreds of creative jamming sessions, producing countless memorable scenes for moviegoers. Raj Kapoor's muse and co-star Nargis also had her own space in the studio for as long as she was part of his life. What was originally Nargis's dressing room was later converted into a somewhat chaotic museum, housing memorabilia from the studio's most iconic films. The umbrella from '*Pyar hua, ikrar hua*', Raj Kapoor's hats from *Shree 420*, Vyjayanthimala's sarees from *Sangam*, Dimple Kapadia's dresses from *Bobby* and several other props were part of this museum.

R.K. Studios was, of course, a prime shooting location for hundreds of Hindi films, not only Raj Kapoor's, and it was a place where history was made. Beyond films, R.K. Studios was an enduring symbol of Bollywood razzmatazz. Apart from the weddings of Raj Kapoor's children and grandchildren,

R.K. Studios hosted Chembur's most famous Ganpati festival and the celebrations ended with the Kapoor family dancing on the streets as their idol left the studio premises. Raj Kapoor's legendary Holi parties were held here – whoever was invited to these festivities was seen as having 'arrived' in Bollywood. The studio's sprawling grounds hosted our cinema's biggest stars dancing and singing with gay abandon, playfully dunking each other in massive tubs, and getting intoxicated with both bhaang and stardust.

In 2017, a devastating fire ripped through R.K. Studios and destroyed a lot of the priceless memorabilia that the museum housed. The rest of the studio could be rebuilt, but this loss was irreplaceable. The Kapoor family probably lost their will to retain the property after this. It was put on the block soon after and – as the prime location and elite history warranted – was sold for a massive undisclosed sum. The gates to a timeless legacy were now closed.

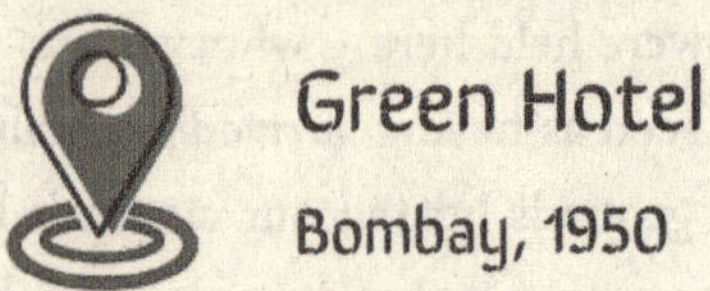

Green Hotel

Bombay, 1950

Sahir Ludhianvi was a legend in Urdu poetry circles when he came to Bombay to become a lyricist. But his reputation – which certainly preceded him – did more harm than good. Film-makers didn't believe a poet of his stature would be able to write filmi ditties, customized to tune and situation. He wrote the songs for a few films, but largely remained unnoticed. His hardship forced him to sell his mother's jewellery, as well as take up some mundane work.

Sachin Dev Burman, meanwhile, had had a moderately successful stint in Calcutta before trying his luck as a composer in Bombay. He was very strong technically, which earned him the respect of singers and musicians, but he hadn't yet caught the nation's fancy. The old guard of the music scene was slowly fading and new talent was emerging. But without a major hit under his belt, S.D. Burman wasn't considered among them yet.

One of Sahir's friends had suggested that he meet Burman – this was when both these extremely talented people were in a similar position in the industry. Sahir went across to Green Hotel in Khar, and walked straight into Burman's room, ignoring the 'Do Not Disturb' sign on the door. Burman, coming from Bengal, had no clue about Sahir's stature as a poet, and was almost relieved to find a potential lyricist walking in unannounced. He explained the situation of the song, played the tune on his harmonium and asked Sahir to come up with lyrics. The creative challenge of the task was daunting, but it was Sahir Ludhianvi sitting at the other end of the harmonium. He asked Burman to play the tune again and, with the music, he came up with '*Thandi hawayein, lehra ke aayein/Rut hai jawaan, tum ho yahaan, kaise bhulayein…*' (which became part of the film *Naujawan*).

It is difficult to say who was happier on discovering the other, but one of Hindi cinema's most productive partnerships were born that day in that hotel. Over the next few years, the Sahir–SD combination pretty much made Dev Anand's career with a succession of massive hit soundtracks – *Baazi, Jaal, Taxi Driver, House No. 44, Funtoosh, Munimji* – that remain popular even today. Legendary directors began taking them on. Bimal Roy's *Devdas* – which had the daunting task of matching up to K.L. Saigal's earlier version – featured them. Guru Dutt's *Pyaasa* was possibly their greatest collaboration, where SD's soaring music framed the scathing commentary on society that Sahir dished out in his lyrics.

Pyaasa was also their swansong. They were two highly talented but temperamental individuals – both convinced about the supremacy of their respective craft. Sahir insisted on taking one rupee more than the fees of composers in his films to establish the primacy of lyrics over music. During the making of *Pyaasa*, an inebriated Sahir said at a gathering that poets were why songs became popular and that composers were lesser mortals. SD got very upset with this statement and refused to work with Sahir any longer. The last song of *Pyaasa* was composed and recorded without the two even sitting together. All good things must come to an end...

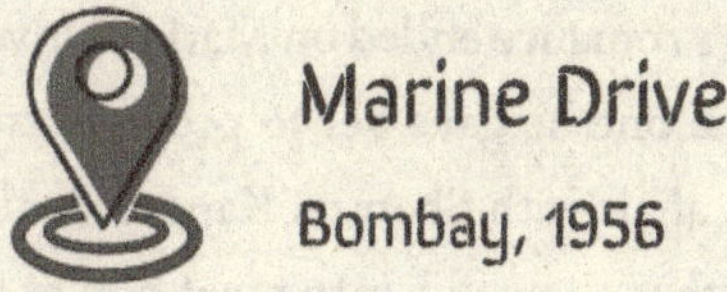

Marine Drive

Bombay, 1956

It is to the Hindi film industry's credit that even a bus conductor could get noticed and land a major part in a film. And it is to his talent's credit that he managed to have a hit song in a major film picturized on him within a few years of entering the movies. So it is quite apt that the song (from *C.I.D.*) picturized on ex-bus conductor Johnny Walker started from one landmark in Bombay (Victoria Terminus) and ended up on another – probably the city's most famous.

Marine Drive – built and enhanced through the 1920s and 1930s – became a popular shooting location early on. Obviously, its wide expanse (with very few cars in the initial days) and uninterrupted view of the sea were big draws. But the real lives of stars also contributed to the allure. Nargis' (or rather, her mother's) apartment – in a building called Chateau Marine – was located here, and this was where her career in films started. Dev Anand and Suraiya's romance ended on Marine Drive when she threw the ring – the one he gave her to profess his love – into the sea. Mumtaz's affair with Shammi Kapoor could have blossomed had her mother allowed her to meet him at (music director) Jaikishan's flat, which was two floors above hers in the same building (Gobind Mahal) on Marine Drive.

Every major star from Rajesh Khanna ('*Zindagi ek safar hai suhana*' in *Andaz*) to Amitabh Bachchan ('*Rote hue aate hain sab*' in *Muqaddar Ka Sikandar*) to Shah Rukh Khan ('*Koi na koi chahiye*' in *Deewana*) announced their ascension to stardom with a hit song pictured along Marine Drive. When Bachchan landed in Bombay with no support whatsoever, he spent several nights on the cement benches dotting the place because he had nowhere else to go. That way, the flamboyant song bookended his stardom very well – from being a nonentity to being the centre of attraction.

Apart from being the location of innumerable songs, Marine Drive became the shorthand for Bombay in Hindi cinema. In a union leader's home in faraway Jharkhand, we see Marine Drive on a wall calendar. The union leader has run away, disgraced by his company's ruthless owners. His family is being victimized and they decided to leave too. The camera zooms on to the sweeping curve, and we see Sumitra, Vijay and Ravi Verma in Bombay – here to rebuild their life in the city of dreams. Vijay soon ascends the high-rise at the end of Marine Drive, and is offered a life of crime and fortune. His decision to take up that offer came from the memory of his family stumbling down Marine Drive when they had lost everything. In a way, the story of *Deewaar* began on Marine Drive.

And if we go back to the song from *C.I.D.*, it can very well be called the theme song of Bombay: '*Ae dil, hai mushkil jeena yahan/Zara hatke, zara bachke, yeh hai Bombay meri jaan…*' For ages, people have come to Bombay, got swindled and nearly left, but stuck on to become successful – gambled and lost, gambled again and won, but never gave up on hard work, never gave up on their dreams. And in this city of dreams, the Queen's Necklace gleams the brightest.

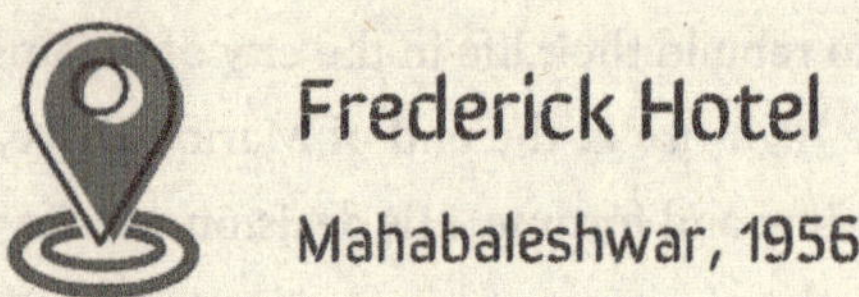

Frederick Hotel

Mahabaleshwar, 1956

Navketan Films had been idle for nearly a year, waiting for Raj Khosla to finalize a script, and Dev Anand was getting jittery about having to pay salaries with no film in sight. Navketan's general manager, Jovilal Parashar, approached Dev and asked him to listen to a script that Vijay Anand had written. Vijay's only condition was that he wanted to direct the film too. Dev was very sceptical about his kid brother (then in his early twenties) helming a film, but grudgingly agreed to a narration. On a weekend drive to Mahabaleshwar, Dev asked Vijay to come along and read out the script. The star offered no reaction after the reading was complete. It was only on reaching Frederick Hotel – his usual stay – that he booked a trunk call to Bombay and instructed his production manager, 'Book Kardar Studios for ten days. Production number 8 has been postponed. We are starting production number 9. Goldie will be directing it.' And Vijay 'Goldie' Anand's directorial career started with *Nau Do Gyarah*.

If there ever was an archetypal wonder-boy in the Hindi film industry, it was Vijay Anand. Youngest of the three incredible Anand brothers, he started imbibing art, culture, film-making and stardom from the people around him even before he hit his teens. But being a lot younger than his two older brothers, he was always diffident about the skills he had to offer. He was only nineteen years old when he wrote the screenplay of *Taxi Driver*. The film became a big hit, but he received neither any money nor praise from his brothers. Vijay had offered the script of *Nau Do Gyarah* first to director Shaheed Latif, but Latif's wife – noted Urdu writer Ismat Chugtai – objected and the project was dropped. Dev took Vijay on as the director only after he heard his assured narration with all the technical details already noted in the script.

Nau Do Gyarah marks the beginning of a stellar career in direction for Vijay Anand. His skills in storytelling, handling actors and song picturization came to the fore, with senior actors, the lyricist (Majrooh Sultanpuri) and the music composer

(S.D. Burman) of the film praising him highly. After it became a hit, he formed a durable partnership with Dev Anand that produced everything from superhits to all-time classics. *Kala Bazar, Tere Ghar Ke Samne, Guide, Jewel Thief* and *Johny Mera Naam* pretty much made Dev Anand's career as a star, and the partnership took a break only when Dev decided to become a director himself (often to disastrous results). Vijay straddled a wide range of roles – acting, writing, editing – beyond direction and became a bona fide legend of Hindi cinema.

He also remained Chetan and Dev Anand's kid brother for a very long time. *Guide*, a script that matched Vijay's skills almost perfectly, came to him only because Chetan left to make another film. *Teesri Manzil,* made under the banner of Nasir Hussain Films, briefly became a question mark for Vijay when Dev walked out of the movie. And, of course, *Nau Do Gyarah* waited for months till Dev could get to a hotel in Mahabaleshwar to listen to his younger brother's script!

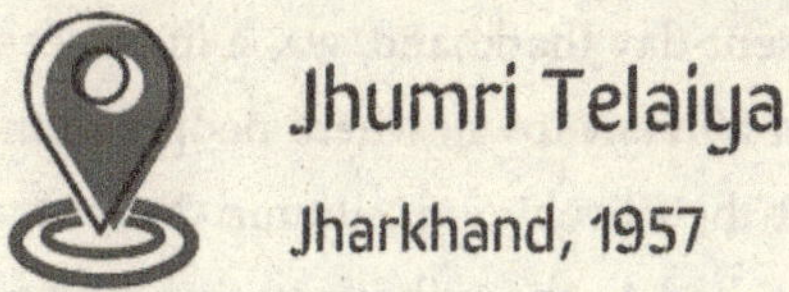

Jhumri Telaiya

Jharkhand, 1957

Before Sudesh Bhosle made his name as a playback singer, his claim to fame was an audio cassette (*Picnic Ke Rang, Sitaron Ke Sang*) in which he mimicked the voices of pretty much every major Bollywood star. In the skit, all these actors were having a ball on their way to a picnic in Jhumri Telaiya. This cassette became a cult favourite, and radio's favourite Jhumri Telaiya got a new lease of life in the world of television.

Jhumri Telaiya has a Timbuktu-like quality to it. It sounds like a fictitious name – more so because it started appearing on radio with a metronomic regularity from the 1950s, its residents putting in requests for songs on both All India Radio and Radio Ceylon. When Ameen Sayani read out a *farmaaish* from 'Rameshwar Prasad Barnwal, Jhumri Telaiya *se*', it just sounded like a place that was invented just to sneak in a fake request! Except that, it was not. It was very real.

Koderma, in present-day Jharkhand, was a major centre for mica mining and an affluent town, where people didn't have to worry a lot about their livelihoods. Jhumri Telaiya was the town that came attached to the railway station of Koderma. From the early 1950s, Hindi songs were super popular on radio, and sending song requests on postcards was quite the thing. It simply exploded when All India Radio started their Vividh Bharati service in 1957.

The aforementioned Rameshwar Barnwal was one of the pioneers of the trend – often sending in several dozen postcards a week with song requests. When *Mughal-e-Azam* was at its peak, his telegram requesting '*Jab pyar kiya toh darna kya*' was read out, interrupting normal programming, and he became something of an icon. Soon, almost the entire town joined in and there was a whole ecosystem that came up to support this pursuit. For starters, the request format was printed on the postcards itself, so that the sender didn't have to go through the trouble of writing 'Film: _____, Song: ______' and other sundry details.

While other towns and villages also started sending requests in droves, none could match Jhumri Telaiya – probably due to the quirky quality of its name. *Hasina Maan Jaayegi* (1968) featured a song that went '*Main Jhumri Telaiya jaoongi, sainyan tore kaaran*' and, 50 years later, *Jagga Jasoos* sang '*Mera gaon Jhumri Telaiya, tera gaon shayad Timbuktu*', and went on to embody the spirit of wishes that the small town started: '*Duniya yeh thodi hai behtar lagey, dil ke naukar chakar lagey, jhuk ke poochhe kya hai arzoo...*'

For Jhumri Telaiya, the *arzoos* were fulfilled on radio every night for a fairly long time.

Asian Games

Tokyo, 1958

In the history of sports, the Asian Games at Tokyo is nothing but a speck of dust. Spanning eight days – from one Sunday to the next – in May and June of 1958, it saw a lacklustre performance from India, who finished seventh in the medal tally. But the games provided a rich haul for Bollywood a few decades later ... *Bhaag Milkha Bhaag* and *Paan Singh Tomar*.

Both Milkha and Paan Singh's careers followed a similar trajectory. Both came from extremely underprivileged backgrounds – Milkha battling the horrific memories of Partition and Paan Singh dealing with debilitating poverty in the Chambal area. Both found jobs in the Army, which provided them a temporary reprieve. Both gravitated towards sports to satiate their ravenous appetite: Only the sportsmen in the armed forces were given unlimited ration! They were spotted almost immediately for their talents and trained for greater things. Milkha found his calling in the shorter distances, especially 200 m and 400 m races. Paan Singh started off with long distance running (5000 m) till he took up 3,000-m steeplechase on his coach's bidding. Ironically, both their fortunes were decided on the use of shoes with spikes. Milkha was introduced to spiked training shoes before the national-level games, while Paan Singh ran in canvas shoes till the National Games of 1958 – where they both broke national records.

Their trajectories started diverging from the 1958 Tokyo Asiad. India won five gold medals here, all of them in athletics. And Milkha Singh won two of them – in 200 m and 400 m races. These victories were the first indications of his exceptional career as an international athlete.

A medal India didn't win was in the 3,000-m steeplechase. Paan Singh's national record in the event was better than the Asian record at that time. But he was given running spikes just before the race, and he couldn't adjust with the new gear, ending up without a medal.

Even accounting for the dramatization that's expected in a film, India's lack of organized preparation was a major reason that Paan Singh Tomar lost out at an international stage, and had to stick to competing at the national level (where he was a seven-time national champion). His lack of recognition caused immense frustration and eventually, led to him rebelling against the system and becoming an outlaw, the focus of his biopic.

Bhaag Milkha Bhaag didn't focus on the 1958 Asiad too much, giving the Rome Olympics and the Indo-Pakistan meet of 1960 more screen time because they were the biggest stages Milkha was part of – both in professional and personal terms.

Be it the glory of Milkha or the downfall of Paan Singh, it was the Tokyo Asiad[4] where the two curves touched each other. And then separated.

---

4. These are not the only stories of the Tokyo Asiad. India – then a major footballing nation – lost to South Korea in the semi-finals of the 1958 Tokyo Asiad. In 1962, they went on to win the Asiad gold... defeating South Korea in the finals. The coach who's widely credited for this victory was Syed Abdul Rahim, to be played by Ajay Devgn in *Maidaan*.

Ajanta Pictures' Studio

Kaagaz Ke Phool, 1959

Cinematographer V.K. Murthy and director Guru Dutt were sitting around in a film set after a day's shooting of *Kaagaz Ke Phool*, when they observed a shaft of sunlight. It was beaming through the hole in the exhaust fan, and the dust particles floating in it created a magical quality. Guru Dutt told Murthy, 'I'll give you 10 days to work out a way of shooting this sunbeam.'[5]

This impulsive, indulgent decision – to include a thing of beauty in the film without a thought – exemplified *Kaagaz Ke*

5. V.K. Murthy's success in pulling this off was rewarded with a Filmfare for Best Cinematography and a legend status in the industry. At the premiere of *Kaagaz Ke Phool*, Shammi Kapoor looked for Murthy, hoisted him up and announced, 'Here is the hero of the film.'

Phool, a resounding flop when it released and a veritable classic when the trade reports ceased to matter. While critics said these indulgences weighed the film down, they went on to become symbols representing the Hindi film industry. The shaft of light was replicated by Murthy, who used two massive mirrors, each about 4-feet tall, placed on the catwalk near the roof of the studio. One mirror was used to reflect sunlight outside on to the second mirror, which was placed at such an angle that it reflected the shaft of light on to the studio floor. It was a pioneering method then, which went on to be extensively used in films. The most famous use of this 'shaft of light' in *Kaagaz Ke Phool* was during the song '*Waqt ne kiya kya haseen sitam*' – a classic created by S.D. Burman and Kaifi Azmi, and brought to life by Guru Dutt and Waheeda Rehman in India's first CinemaScope film, seen as an extravagant waste then.

Kaagaz Ke Phool was largely seen as Guru Dutt's own version of his life. Legendary director Suresh Sinha (played by Guru Dutt) – prime mover of Ajanta Pictures – discovers stars, makes classics and resists artistic compromises, till his films flop and he is hounded out of the studio he built. The studio is the centre of his universe and thus, the film's. Ajanta Pictures is where he immerses himself in his work, losing his wife and daughter in the process. It is also the source of his angst, because his in-laws don't see his profession as an honourable one. It is also the place where he finds his muse – played by Waheeda Rehman, in yet another autobiographical touch – when she accidentally walks on to a set in the studio and gets captured on film. He casts her as Paro in *Devdas* – another tragic hero's tale – despite opposition from his associates, and she becomes a star. *Kaagaz Ke Phool* was eerily prophetic because when it was made, Guru Dutt was fresh off the critical and commercial success of *Pyaasa*. However, with its failure, he spiralled into debt and fell into a mental abyss that he never really recovered from. He refused to direct his subsequent films, and eventually, died young and alone, five years later.

Much like Raj Kapoor seeing himself as a joker and making an overlong ode to a circus in *Mera Naam Joker*, Guru Dutt saw himself at home in a film studio and feared – as in the film – of dying unsung. *Kaagaz Ke Phool* starts with an aged Dutt feeling his way around the deserted studio, and ends with him dead in a director's chair – placed in a beam of sunlight. And, in a poignant end, he comes face to face with his muse, who's now a star, while he is reduced to an 'extra' – in the same studio. As he runs away from her, she follows him, but can't catch up because she's mobbed by fans. As the song went, '*Tum rahe na tum, hum rahe na hum…*'

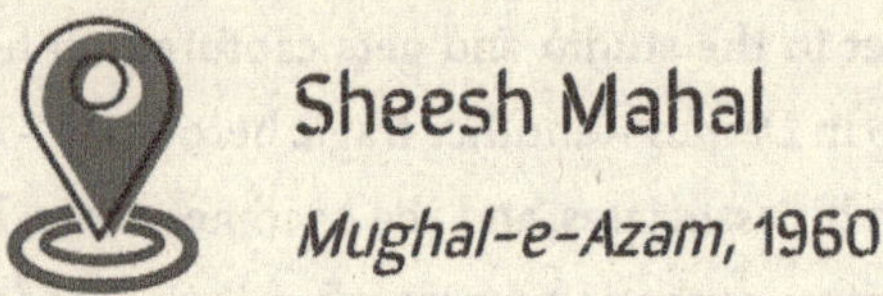

Sheesh Mahal

Mughal-e-Azam, 1960

'*Theek hai, seth, jo tumhari marzi ho, karo; magar ek baat sun lo – yeh set main hi mukammal karoonga.* Film *ka baaki kaam kisi se bhi mukammal kara lena, magar is* set *par koi doosra* director *aaya toh main us ki taang tod doonga,*' K. Asif told his producer, Shapoorji Pallonji (the construction tycoon), standing in what was the most expensive Hindi film set at the time. And this incident was emblematic of Asif's passion and extravagance in the making of *Mughal-e-Azam*. He wanted the best of the best, and was ready to pay higher than the highest to get just that. Composer Naushad Ali said that Asif came to him with ₹1 lakh in cash to sign him up for the film and remained unperturbed when Naushad threw the money away. And it started from there. From getting Ustad Bade Ghulam Ali Khan to be the voice of Tansen, to commissioning shoes for Akbar that cost thousands of rupees, he left no stone unturned to give his film that legendary Mughal flair.

The epitome of this quest was the Sheesh Mahal set, in which the legendary '*Pyar kiya toh darna kya*' song was performed. The set was 30-feet high, 80-feet wide and 150-feet long. Artisans from Firozabad (known for glass handicraft) were brought in to embed lakhs of small circular mirrors into the walls, pillars and ceiling. This set took nearly two years to construct. Asif wanted it so grand because it was going to be the only colour sequence in the black-and-white film.

Conventional wisdom said that it was impossible to film in a hall full of mirrors... How would the camera not be seen? Won't the reflecting lights create an impossible glare? How can so many heavy mirrors be supported by a temporary structure? But Asif seemed to blow away all doomsday prophesies with his cigarette smoke. And his ingenuity. He applied a light coat of wax on the mirrors to reduce the reflection.

The set was so expensive that his producer threatened to throw him out of the film – in an altercation that took place on that set itself – and wanted Sohrab Modi to complete the film. Asif retorted that it was a matter of honour for him to shoot this song, as it was the only way to prove the industry wrong. He offered to quit once he completed shooting the song. Eventually, the footage was sent to Technicolor in London to get it reviewed by experts, who were impressed enough to telegram a congratulatory message back. And even Shapoorji forgot his own reservations when he saw the rushes, and not only kept Asif on but increased budgets for the scenes he shot later.

Mughal-e-Azam represents the Grand Bollywood Film perfectly – Over-the-top sets, an enormous budget, memorable dialogues and unforgettable acting. In the Sheesh Mahal, K. Asif played all aspects of the sequence – from the budget to the music to the words to the performance to the costumes to the set design – like a master conductor guides an orchestra to play a symphony. And the Sheesh Mahal became a place where Bollywood dreams got made.

A young lawyer reaches a moneylender's home on a personal matter, when another visitor walks in. The lawyer hides in the adjoining room and sees the visitor murdering the moneylender. He recognizes the murderer, but keeps quiet – at least initially. Not only because the moneylender's death solves several of his personal problems, but also because the murderer is his would-be father-in-law. And also happens to be the judge presiding over the trial for murder.

B.R. Chopra's *Kanoon* was path-breaking because it was a songless legal thriller. The thriller genre wasn't new to Hindi cinema, neither was a courtroom scene with impressive dialogues, but not having songs was unprecedented in Hindi cinema. (About a decade later, B.R. Chopra produced and his brother, Yash, directed another songless thriller, *Ittefaq*, starring Rajesh Khanna, before the star became a sensation.)

Dev Anand had played a lawyer in *Aandhiyan*; Nargis played one in *Awara*. In both films, the legal tangle was restricted to a relatively smaller part of the script, and neither film could be called a 'legal thriller'. *Kanoon*, on the other hand, is placed entirely in the legal world. Two judges discuss the moral problem of capital punishment and whether one can actually commit the perfect murder. The prosecution and defence's cases are meticulously built, with both parties diligently finding weaknesses in the reasonings. And beyond the legal tangles, it also tried to resolve the moral dilemma of protecting (or not) a man – a mentor, a well-respected pillar of society – from being implicated in the murder of a despicable character.

Despite the lack of traditionally entertaining elements, *Kanoon* managed to draw a reasonable crowd, thanks to its star cast. There is a twist in the end that would go on to inspire legal thrillers in the future, as lawyers turn quasi-detectives and solve the mystery behind whatever soup their client land in.

Rajendra Kumar and Ashok Kumar were pitted against each other, though not as arguing attorneys. Rajendra Kumar's sincere looks and deliberate dialogue-delivery style established him as the perfect lawyer – a template for several lawyer characters in the future. On the other hand, Ashok Kumar was at his suave best – playing the judge who didn't seem to be all that perturbed by a potential murder charge against him.

When a court wants to protect intellectual property (a film, a show, a book) against an anonymous person or group of people, they issue – what is called – a 'John Doe order'. Often before the release of a high-profile movie, courts issue a John Doe order, prohibiting potential pirates from illegally distributing the content. In India, a 'John Doe order' is also called an 'Ashok Kumar order'. And fans of Hindi cinema can be forgiven for thinking it is because of *Kanoon*.

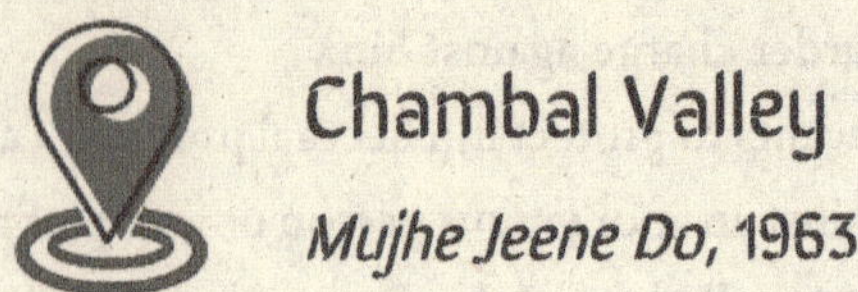

Chambal Valley

***Mujhe Jeene Do*, 1963**

In May 1960, noted Gandhian Vinoba Bhave addressed a public meeting on the banks of Chambal River, and made an appeal to the fearsome dacoits of the area to surrender and assimilate into society. This brought back the dacoits – whose presence in the Chambal valley is part of Indian folklore – into the limelight, and several films about them were made in quick succession. *Jis Desh Mein Ganga Behti Hai* and *Ganga Jumna* released in 1960–1961, featuring two of Hindi cinema's biggest names – Raj Kapoor and Dilip Kumar respectively – and were big hits, with *Ganga Jumna* being counted as one of the all-time classics of Hindi cinema.

Mujhe Jeene Do is lesser known as a film, but stands out from other dacoit films for the realistic portrayal of their lives. And this wasn't merely the assessment of critics or audiences. Journalist and film expert Deepak Mahaan interviewed some former dacoits, who were 'near unanimous that *Mujhe Jeene Do* had the most authentic depiction of dacoits' lives'. One of them – while recounting an escape from the police – said that it was similar to a scene in *Mujhe Jeene Do*.

The realism came from the partnership of director Moni Bhattacharjee (an assistant to Bimal Roy on films like *Do Bigha Zamin* and *Madhumati*) and producer–actor Sunil Dutt (who was unflinching in his choice of socially relevant cinema). *Mujhe Jeene Do* is the story of a dacoit leader Jarnail Singh (Dutt), who's ruthless to begin with, but repents after he falls in love with a courtesan (Waheeda Rehman) and has a son. The cycle of retribution comes a full circle when he shoots down a morally upright villager in the opening scene, and now must seek shelter in the same village for his family.

Unlike most dacoit films which depend on sets and sterile outdoor locations, *Mujhe Jeene Do* was almost entirely shot in the Bhind and Morena districts of Madhya Pradesh. The opening message of the film thanks the villagers of Nagra, Kanera, Dhurra and Porsa, and has a heartfelt word for the Madhya Pradesh

Police. 'All of us will treasure the memory of the days we spent with the officers and jawans who face hardships and death every day with incredible cheerfulness and courage...' *Mujhe Jeene Do* is a rare Hindi film which worked on both commercial and critical fronts. It was one of the biggest hits of the year, and was one of the few Indian films to be sent to the Cannes Film Festival, in competition for the Palme d'Or.

It also established the Robin Hood–like appeal of dacoits in Hindi cinema. They were always honourable people forced by circumstances to take to the gun. Dacoit films continued to be a popular genre well into the 1990s – though much of it had degenerated into action and sleaze fests. Dacoit films have died out in the new millennium, though the best explanation of the dacoits' enduring appeal came from a recent film. Differentiating dacoits from criminals, Paan Singh Tomar said, '*Beehad mein baaghi hote hai; dacait milte hain* Parliament *mein.*'

Europe

Sangam, 1964

'Ageless as Asia, Exciting as Europe,' the posters screamed, and the excitement of Raj Kapoor shooting a colour film for the first time was palpable. Add to that the fact that it was the first Hindi film to have been shot extensively in Europe, and *Sangam* was a superhit even before it released.

War hero Sundar (Raj Kapoor) is posted to London just before his marriage, and he goes off on an extended honeymoon to all the major European capitals with his bride, Vyjayanthimala. The film then brought in the melodrama of a love triangle, but its predictability was rescued by the superhit music and an unprecedented view of the world's most famous tourist attractions. The couple start by seeing the Big Ben in London, go on to throw a coin in the Trevi Fountain in Rome, take motorboat and gondola rides on the canals of Venice, visit the top tier of the Eiffel Tower in Paris and finally end by rolling on the snow-covered mountains of Switzerland. This whole segment lasted nearly an hour (in a film that ran for nearly four hours, with two intervals). It included two songs, of which one said '*I love you*' in German, French and Russian, apart from its message of international brotherhood.

Sangam was the biggest box-office hit of the year, and one of the most successful films of the 1960s. And it started a trend. Phrases like 'visual seduction' and 'dripping with glamour' laced the descriptions, and the Indian audiences were keen to sample more of this. In the next few years, a slew of big-budget films were shot in Europe, with a high degree of technical finesse that matched the locations' grandeur. Films like *Love in Tokyo, An Evening in Paris, Night in London* and *Around the World* created a flutter till shooting abroad wasn't a novelty anymore; and then a second wave was started by Yash Chopra in the 1980s.

When Raj Kapoor was asked at a press conference in London why he shot such a large part of the film in Europe, his answer was as practical as it was prescient. 'Because it was a fresh new locale. [Also] there are so many Indians living abroad today... They carry our culture with them and merge it in the wider context of Western living. It is significant that in this film I wanted to achieve a similar merging. It is not for nothing that this film is entitled *Sangam*.' He had accentuated the allure of the foreign locations by punching in desi *sanskar* at the right moments. Vyjayanthimala wears sarees, covers her head and refuses to be kissed in public places. In Paris, she stops her husband from going to a cabaret show. When challenged, she puts up a show herself, rivalling the best of what Paris has to offer. Thus becoming the perfect desi wife: Sexy, yet sanskari. Raj Kapoor had targeted the NRI market, 30 years before Bollywood was given credit for it.

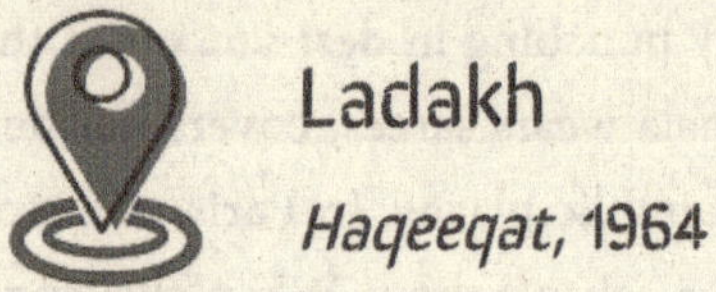

Ladakh

Haqeeqat, 1964

Director Chetan Anand went to Ladakh about a year after the 1962 Sino-Indian war. He wanted to make 'India's first war film' and shot nearly 1-lakh feet of footage of Ladakh's breathtaking beauty. He neither had a story nor the finances to make such an audacious film. He came back to Bombay to write the script after this recce. Anand formed his production company – Himalaya Pictures – and secured funding from the government of Punjab to make the film. He was supposed to direct the prestigious Indo-American co-production, *Guide,* starring his brother Dev, but exited the production to make *Haqeeqat* – the first film to be shot in Ladakh. Which, by all accounts, proved very difficult to make.

Writing a script on a war India lost is no easy feat. *Haqeeqat* focuses on the micro-unit of war, and is about a battalion stuck in Ladakh in the face of the advancing Chinese army. They initially make fun of the relentless Chinese broadcasts asking them to surrender, then they are irritated, and finally, they realize they are hopelessly outnumbered. It is the story of their outstanding valour in an unequal battle. The tone of the film is best captured by the iconic song from the film, '*Kar chale hum fida jaan-o-tan saathiyon, ab tumhare hawale watan saathiyon*'.

Haqeeqat gives a glimpse of the failing Indian diplomacy and military leadership by showing how the forces were ordered not to shoot at the enemy for an untenably long period. The humanity of the army comes out through subplots about a captain falling in love with a local girl, and other soldiers yearning for home and family. One soldier receives seeds and saplings from home, so that he can plant them in his camp and get a glimpse of his village.

This subplot is especially ironic because the location is the barren mountainscape, where no vegetation exists for miles. The cold desert is a metaphor for the Indian soldier – caught between an unrelenting enemy and a dithering leadership. The location of Ladakh was recreated by the stunning work of cinematographer Sadanand and art director M.S. Sathyu. The authenticity was maintained even in the sets that were recreated in Bombay's Mehboob Studio. But the cast and crew shot parts of the film in extremely harsh conditions, to make the film realistic. Much of the cold-related inflictions – burnt skin, chapped lips – we see on the actors of the film were real, not requiring make-up.

The publicity campaign for *Haqeeqat* said, 'The Chinese attack started in waves, from another direction, and from many other directions… The many that attacked, the few that defended'. Posters and ads showed the wide vistas of Ladakh with uncountable Chinese soldiers swamping the mountains. Ladakh eventually became a tourist magnet (aided by glamourous shoots of Bollywood in the 1990s and 2000s). But in 1962, it was the place where thousands of brave Indian soldiers were slaughtered, their blood staining the grim visage of the mountains.

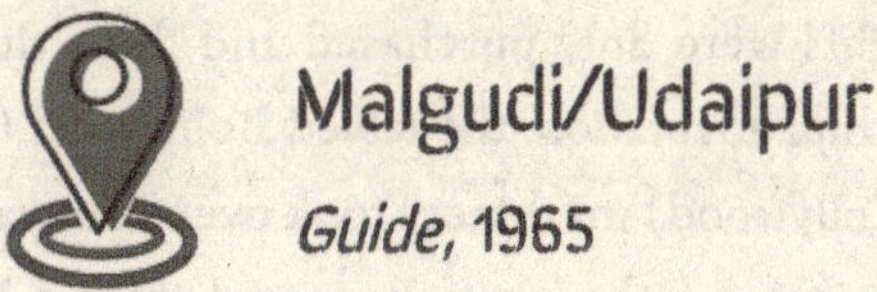

Malgudi/Udaipur

Guide, 1965

Dev Anand's enthusiastic recounting of the making of his film *Guide* and author R.K. Narayan's sardonic retelling of the same incidents based on his novel *The Guide* couldn't be more different. While Dev Anand imagined a reclusive author impressed by his showbiz credentials, Narayan was passing trenchant comments on the extravagant frivolity of Bollywood folks.

R.K. Narayan's classic novel came into the picture when Dev Anand decided to co-produce a film (with American director Ted Danielewski and Nobel Prize–winning author Pearl S. Buck) that would be made in both English and Hindi. The English version was to have a fully Indian cast in an Indian story made for an international audience. The story was the simple tale of an extramarital love between an unscrupulous guide, Raju, and a dancer, Rosie – set in Malgudi, like all of Narayan's works.

After the rights were duly purchased and the writer was assured of a faithful adaptation, the fabled Bollywood (and in this case, also Hollywood) machinery took over. Narayan took a reconnaissance crew to the locations in and around Mysore which had inspired the locales and characters of his book *The Guide*. The Kaveri River, forest bungalows, small shrines, temples on riverbanks and annual religious fairs were all there – exactly as described in the book. The crew took down meticulous notes. And then decided to shoot the film mostly in Jaipur and Udaipur.

Shooting for the first time in India using Eastmancolor film meant the production needed a spectacle, and they created one! Dev Anand spent ₹2 lakhs – an astronomical sum for the times – on costumes alone. Two cameras, fifteen arc lamps, a thousand yards of electric wiring and a 100-yard wooden platform were assembled in Udaipur for the shoot. For a nine-minute long dance sequence (in the song '*Piya tose naina laaga re*'), nine sets were created. The story changed a fair bit too. The book's Bharatanatyam performer became a dancer in the popular mould of Hindi cinema. The casual, sexual nature of the adulterous liaison between Raju and Rosie in the book became a justified elopement from an abusive and philandering husband. And all the locales that could have been naturally found in South India were recreated in various parts of North and West India.

This is not to say the Hindi film was poorly made – in fact, far from it. It had some great dance spectacles, a lovely soundtrack that has stood the test of time and strong acting. It has often been hailed a classic in Hindi cinema. Even R.K. Narayan told writer–director Vijay Anand that his script was stronger than the story. Except that it was not R.K. Narayan's *Guide*; it was Vijay Anand's *Guide*.

Satyajit Ray was also impressed by R.K. Narayan's book, but had felt that he would not be able to recreate the South Indian milieu of Malgudi that was so integral to the story, and passed over the opportunity to make a film. The Bollywoods operate differently, and, in a commercial film shoot, the intimacy of emotions often gives way to the grandness of spectacles – though that is not always a bad thing. *Guide* won all the major prizes at the Filmfare Awards that year, including the Best Story prize for R.K. Narayan.

Rekha and Jagmohan's Home

Ittefaq, 1969

The shooting of *Aadmi Aur Insaan* ran into an unexpected hitch just two weeks before completion. Heroine Saira Banu fell ill and had to go to London for a month for her treatment. Yash Chopra's assistant director on *Waqt*, Mahen Vakil, took him and producer B.R. Chopra to see a Gujarati play. The play, *Dhummas*, was based on an English play – *Signpost to Murder* by Monte Doyle. The tight thriller impressed the Chopra brothers enough to produce it in their enforced break.

Ittefaq was conceived as a songless thriller – yet another one from B.R. Films, after *Kanoon* – shot in one start-to-finish schedule. The film's screenplay was adapted by Akhtar ul-Iman in just eight days from the script of the play, and the entire movie was shot in only 28 days at Rajkamal Studios. This whole endeavour was a radical departure from the usual workings of the film industry of the 1960s, in which star availability, music recording, shooting, editing and dubbing could literally take years. Even the star availability factor was short-circuited when Yash Chopra's first choices of Shashi Kapoor and Rakhee were not available, and were replaced by Rajesh Khanna and Nanda.

In *Ittefaq*, Rajesh Khanna plays a man accused of murder, on the run from a mental health institution. He barges into a house to hide, and takes the lady (Nanda) hostage. The duo start playing a game of cat and mouse till they seemingly develop feelings for each other. But it soon becomes clear that we don't know who is the cat and who is the mouse. Over the course of one rainy evening and night, a dead body appears and vanishes, suspects vanish and appear as we hurtle towards a – till then in Bollywood, unprecedented – climax.

The majority of the film takes place in just one set – the couple's home. The drawing room and the stairs going up to a mezzanine floor became a surprisingly versatile location for the action, with doors left ajar and open windows playing their part in unravelling the mystery.

Ittefaq released just before *Aradhana*, which would make Rajesh Khanna a superstar – and the two roles cannot be more different. As a murderer who seems to have lost his mental balance, Rajesh Khanna is top notch in *Ittefaq*. He occasionally exaggerates the clichéd mannerisms of mental illness, but his dialogue delivery is sharp and on point. Nanda wears her tension and sensuousness lightly, as the housewife who isn't happy to have an intruder in her home – for more reasons than one.

Ittefaq had a moderate run that recovered its modest budget, but its impact is quite far-reaching. *Star and Style* called it 'the most important film of the year'. As a claustrophobic thriller set almost entirely in one location, it was way ahead of its times and the films it inspired came several decades later. Ram Gopal Verma's *Kaun* also had a woman alone in a house being intruded upon, which had a twist of its own. And B.R. Chopra's grandson, Abhay Chopra, remade the film – setting it on a rainy evening nearly 50 years after the original. To paraphrase Hitchcock, it brought murder to where it belongs – back into the home.

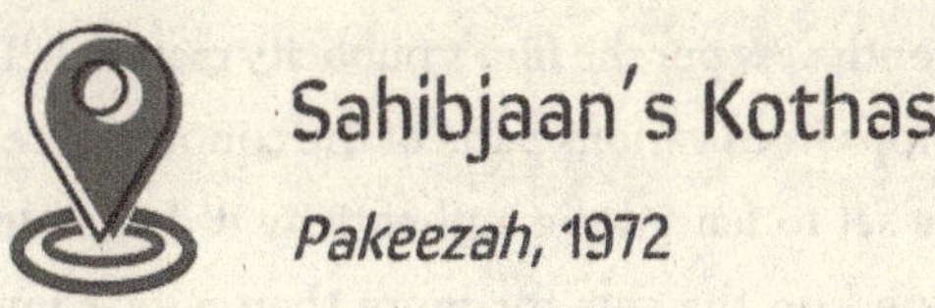

Sahibjaan's Kothas

***Pakeezah*, 1972**

'*Innhi logon ne le li na dupatta mera,*' sang Sahibjaan (Meena Kumari) with gay abandon in her first performance as a courtesan. She was performing for a group of lecherous admirers, inside her kotha in Delhi's Bazaar-e-Husn. This hit song and Meena Kumari's memorable performance was filmed in Bombay's Filmistan Studios – on a set symbolic of the film's grandeur and complexity. In a rare instance of deep-focus photography in Hindi cinema, the sequence had the entire red-light district operating in the background of the song. You can count eight *mujra* performances happening in other buildings, each complete with performers and audiences. Hundreds of dancers were trained for the picturization of the mujras. Apart from that, people are seen walking around, going in and out of shops and establishments. The four-storey set cost over ₹10 lakh and was built by 600 men, working on it round the clock for over eight months. As per the film's publicity material, 'Dozens of genuine shops from various parts of the country were bodily shifted to the set to lend it the authenticity it demanded. The shops remained on the sets for more than a year involving payment of huge compensation to their owners.'

The film moves from Delhi to Lucknow with Sahibjaan and her entourage. The two kothas were the locations for most of the action, and the director, Kamal Amrohi, designed them in loving and meticulous detail. Along with art director N.B. Kulkarni, Amrohi sketched all the set designs and even planned the camera movements within the sets. The Lucknow kotha – called Gulabi Mahal in the film – was decked with curtains, chandeliers, fountains and marbled floors. Some chandeliers were imported from Belgium, while some were bought from the palaces of maharajas. The huge carpet was woven specifically for the film, by dozens of master artists. Amrohi – in an unspoken rivalry with K. Asif – was trying to upstage *Mughal-e-Azam* in grandeur and craft.

Pakeezah was the epitome of the chaos and the passion that goes into the making of the classics of Hindi cinema. It was 15 years in the making – technical challenges, a failed marriage and even a fatal disease could not stop it from being made. The film moved from black and white to colour, from regular to CinemaScope – both changes necessitating reshooting the earlier portions. Director Kamal Amrohi and lead actress Meena Kumari separated as a couple, and were brought back by friends and well-wishers in order to complete the film. Meena Kumari battled a debilitating cirrhosis of the liver and just about completed the film before she passed away (less than two months after its release). And accepted just one gold coin as her remuneration.

Kamal Amrohi and Meena Kumari's romance started from Poona's Sassoon Hospital where they first met, while she was recuperating from an accident and ended on the sets on *Pakeezah*. Amrohi offered to divorce Kumari if she completed *Pakeezah,* his dream project. It seems he was willing to let go of his personal ego for his professional one and created a magnum opus that ended up becoming her swansong. As his publicity manager said, 'Shah Jahan made Taj Mahal for his wife. Kamal sahab wanted to do the same with *Pakeezah.*'

Graveyard

Do Gaz Zameen Ke Neeche, 1972

After watching *Do Gaz Zameen Ke Neeche*, director Ram Gopal Varma was returning home in a bus when he suddenly remembered that his usual stop would mean having to walk through a graveyard to get home. He decided to get off at another stop and walk two kilometres; this way, he didn't have to cross the cemetery! Varma himself went on to make several horror films, and remains a staunch fan of the Ramsay Brothers – India's horror film factory!

Simply put, *Do Gaz Zameen Ke Neeche* was 'India's first horror film'.[6] The plot is part-zombie, part-ghost, a scary premise

---

6. This is slightly debatable, but only due to the Ramsays themselves. Their first venture was a Sindhi horror film, *Naqli Shaan*, made a year earlier.

punched with romance, bathing and bedroom scenes – stuff usually not found in regular Hindi films of the day. (This earned the film an 'Adults Only' rating, but didn't impact its box-office performance.) The film is about a scientist–millionaire, who saves a woman from rape and then marries her, only to realize his wife and her accomplices are out to kill him and take over his property. He is soon 'killed' and buried *do gaz,* i.e. two yards, under the ground. Except that these things never go as they are planned. (The film was loosely based on a story narrated by Asha – the sister of the Ramsay brothers.)

The eponymous grave was in Mahabaleshwar, and the shoot had all the hallmarks of future Ramsay Brothers' productions. They hired their only location – the governor's bungalow in Mahabaleshwar – at ₹500 per day, and actively used the wilderness around the place as well as a nearby graveyard. The priest of a nearby church gave them permission to use the cemetery, and they took the help of locals to identify spots where they could dig without disturbing those buried there.

The graveyard and its attendant chills – a standard horror film trope – would become a Ramsay Brothers' staple as well, more so after the runaway success of *Do Gaz Zameen Ke Neeche.* Made on a shoestring budget, the film made 3–10x of its budget (as per different estimates) and kickstarted the Ramsay juggernaut. The

Ramsays were the pioneers of and had a near monopoly in the horror genre in India. They churned out films at a hectic pace, all of which found a loyal audience looking for chills, thrills and titillations. Films like *Hotel*, *Purana Mandir* (their biggest hit), *3D Saamri*, *Veerana*, *Bandh Darwaza* and *Shaitani Ilaaka* made decent money for their makers, and still have a cult following among people passionate about – what is derogatorily called – 'B-grade movies'. They went into satellite television too, when it launched in India, with *Zee Horror Show*.

The Ramsays are synonymous with horror films in India – probably more than any other producer's association with any other genre. Years later, one of the brothers – Keshu Ramsay – branched out into other productions independently. He produced all five *Khiladi* films (starring Akshay Kumar) and *Khakee* (with an all-star cast). But he always used only his first name in the films' credits and publicity material. Because his surname would make audiences think that these were horror films. To think that a movie starring Amitabh Bachchan, Akshay Kumar, Ajay Devgn and Aishwarya Rai ran the risk of being seen as horror only because of the producer's surname... That's the power of Ramsay! And that graveyard.

An early poster of where it all started… six feet under.

Image courtesy of the Ramsay family

Ramgarh

Sholay, 1975

A village located between ravines. Overlooked by a Thakur's house on a rocky plateau. A central chowk for assembly and celebrations. A towering water tank with a ladder. A mango orchard providing shelter for the sleepy. A Shiva temple and a mosque for the devout. Serviced by a railway station about an hour away. Nearby villages included Belapur, Naopur, Fatehgarh, Haripur and Pipri. Meerut and Moradabad were the nearest 'big cities'.

The geography of *Sholay* is imprinted in millions of Indians' minds. The film had become a cultural milestone for many people growing up in the 1970s to the 1990s, and, from repeated viewings, Ramgarh is a place we have visited countless times.

This place originated from Ramesh Sippy's brief to his art director, Ram Yedekar, that his dacoit film will not be set in the ravines of Chambal. He wanted his film to look nothing like anything seen in Hindi films till then. Yedekar set off in his car from Mumbai, and drove down Maharashtra and well into Karnataka. About an hour out of Bangalore, he found a place with an undulating rocky terrain and huge boulders (which he vaguely remembered from an American film he was part of). The place was called Ramanagaram.

After Ramesh Sippy and cinematographer Dwarka Divecha visited and loved the place, Ramanagaram started becoming Ramgarh with the help of a crew of a hundred people. A semi-permanent village – with nearly 60 houses and other public structures – was built over two months for about four months of continuous shooting. The make-up rooms and bathrooms were located inside villagers' houses, massive godowns and kitchens were built to feed the crew. Even a road was constructed to connect Ramanagaram with the highway. The shooting started with Jai returning the keys to the safe to Radha, and ended with Jai's death scene – the unrequited love story bookending the shoot at the magnificent set. The locals named the place Sippy Nagar (or Sippy Nagaram), given the income the shoot generated for them.

Like most extravagant films, *Sholay* had its naysayers. What G.P. Sippy was doing by putting up a massive set somewhere in South India was beyond most industry pundits and that probably could have weighed on the father–son duo's minds during the shoot. But if it did, there was no sign of it. There was no hesitation in the way they spent money, strategized, and went into a hyper-creative zone to produce probably the most recognizable set in the history of Hindi cinema. The grey vistas, the familiar village landmarks, the paths, the bridges, the water tank, the lake – it all seems organic enough to become a part of our growing up years. Forty years after the movie, when Google released a much-loved ad film about the most recognizable places of Hindi cinema, another father–son duo visited Ramanagaram and the familiar *Sholay* theme music kicked in, taking us all back in time. The place is now called *Sholay* Rocks. Indeed, *Sholay* still rocks.

Film City

Bombay, 1977

When Yash Chopra took on Salim–Javed's script based on the infamous mining accident in Chasnala (now located in Jharkhand), the original plan was to shoot in actual coal mines near Asansol and Dhanbad. But the logistics of shooting so far away kept them in Bombay – choosing instead to create sets of the interiors of mines in a brand-new facility located on the then outskirts of the city. *Kaala Patthar* became the first film to be shot in Film City, even before it was formally inaugurated.

Film City was envisaged as a massive shooting complex – something like a one-stop shop for locations, props, costumes, talent and everything that's needed for shooting a film. It was built by the Government of Maharashtra's Department of

Cultural Affairs on persuasion of film industry doyens like Dilip Kumar, B.R. Chopra and V. Shantaram. Spread over 500 acres of land, Film City claims to have 44 different outdoor locations. This marketing claim seems somewhat subdued because pretty much every single temple, tunnel, haveli, hill station, palace, police station, restaurant, railway station, jail and jungle seen in a Hindi film since the early 1980s is likely to be located here.

In *Kuch Kuch Hota Hai*, Shah Rukh Khan and Rani Mukerji meet at a temple, which is one of the most popular locations in Film City. Even the New York neighbourhood where Preity Zinta and Shah Rukh Khan live in *Kal Ho Naa Ho* was created inside Film City. In between these two Dharma productions, the Chandni Chowk of *Kabhi Khushi Kabhie Gham* was built here after Karan Johar and his team failed to find shooting-friendly locations in the real Chandni Chowk. And not only Delhi, *Devdas*'s Kolkata and *Mission Kashmir*'s Kashmir were both located in Film City. Vidhu Vinod Chopra shot some critical parts of *1942: A Love Story* in Dalhousie's Sadar Bazar, and art director Nitin Desai then recreated the movie's fictitious town in Film City at a cost of ₹80 lakh. There is a lake inside, around which the mini city was created and Maharashtra became Himachal Pradesh for a few months. In an interesting twist, Chopra stayed inside the make-up rooms of Film City for 32 days because he had a dispute with a film-making body and they had decided not to let him enter the complex. So he never left till his shooting was complete. Anil Kapoor shooting for *1942* at Film City is a continuation of a superstition he holds close. The actor shot potions of his first superhit, *Woh 7 Din*, at Film City. Since then, Kapoor insists on shooting for at least one day at Film City for all his films.

In Farah Khan's *Om Shanti Om*, the sprawling RC Studios – which was the centre of all the action in the movie – was actually created in Film City. And, much like in the film, the real place is a factory of dreams.

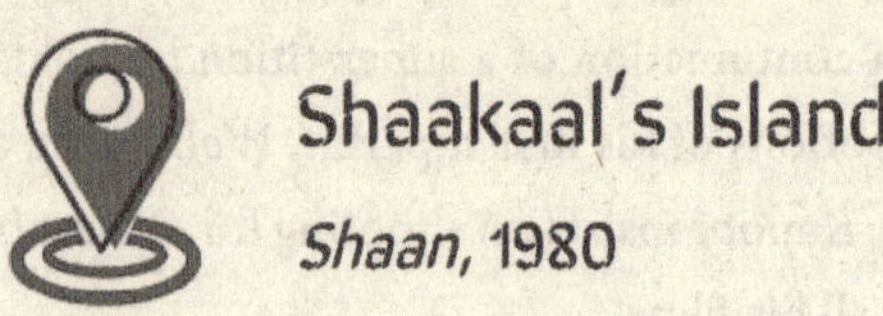

Shaakaal's Island

Shaan, 1980

'*Bambai se teen sau meel door, ek jazeere mein hain… Aur yahaan sawaal poochne ka haq sirf mujhko hai,*' says super villain Shaakaal in his trademark style of chewing on the words before spitting them out. One hour into *Shaan*, we were given a glimpse of the island in the middle of the ocean – accessible only by helicopter.

And this island houses his main hideout, which you reach via an elevator. An army of uniformed, gun-toting male guards and mini-skirted female guards protect the maze of automatic doors and polished floors that lead to the sanctum sanctorum of Shaakaal. A window opens into the ocean outside, and you can see sharks and stingrays swimming about. There are ducts of poisonous gas and a rotating conference table. And under the table, a crocodile lies waiting to devour traitors who will soon come toppling in. Much like his spiritual predecessor Gabbar Singh, Shaakaal also plays a game of Russian roulette with his henchmen. Only his hideout afforded a more high-tech version. And like any self-respecting supervillain hideout, this one too had a self-destruct mode and explodes in a grand heap just as Shaakaal's enemies escape in the nick of time.

At the time of its production, *Sholay* was the most expensive film made. It cost ₹3 crore and grossed an eye-popping ₹25 crore in its very first run – making it the highest-grossing film till then. With *Shaan*, the Sippys pulled out all stops to make a film that was going to be even bigger than their previous one. This was both the strength and weakness of *Shaan*. It was made at a cost of ₹6 crore and made a very creditable ₹12 crore at the box office. (Though, the trade pundits – shaking their heads – had said, 'It isn't *Sholay*.')

The scale of *Shaan* could be seen in the island which was a lot farther away from Bombay than 300 miles. It is called Steep Holm, located in the Bristol Channel, approximately midway between the English counties of Somerset and Glamorgan. With a largely (carboniferous) limestone soil, the island's sides were unusually light grey and provided a unique backdrop to the incoming helicopters and exploding action.

In an industry often reviled for tacky production values, Ramesh Sippy set out to make a James Bond–style caper, and that ambition is visible right from the opening credits with its slinky dance to the villain who – with a bald head – was the spitting image of Ernst Stavro Blofeld, Bond's long-time nemesis. And his den – which outdid even some of the lairs of Bond baddies – is probably the most lavish villain's den in Hindi cinema. And maybe the most excessive as well.

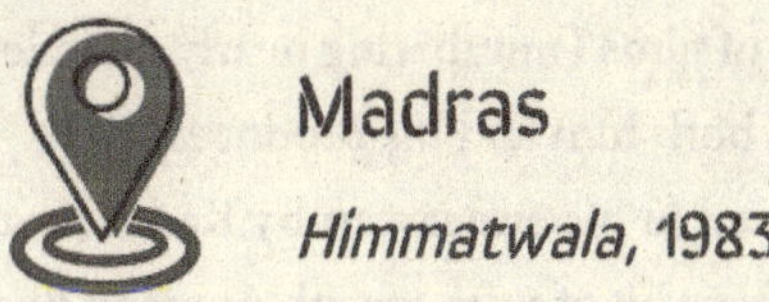

Madras

Himmatwala, 1983

In the first scene of *Himmatwala*, Jeetendra gets off a train with a yellow suitcase and makes his way towards Ramnagar village, with a woman in red ghaghra–choli walking ahead of him. He soon meets Sridevi in a shiny black, all-leather outfit, with a golden cummerbund. The first five minutes of this superhit perfectly showcases the visual aesthetic of the 'Madras' films. (The term 'Madras' is as per the Bollywood worldview, for both Tamil and Telugu films were being remade there.)

Jeetendra moved to the South to avert a personal financial crisis. His home production, *Deedar-e-Yaar*, had turned out to be an expensive flop and he needed a steady income to pay off his debts. South Indian film-makers adhered to schedules, released films well within budget, and paid their actors and crew on time. Jeetendra practically moved to Madras and churned out an assembly line of films (numbering nearly 60 in less than a decade) that made both him and his producers rich.

Jeetendra was joined in his endeavour by Kader Khan, who moved southwards after a bit of a run-in with Amitabh Bachchan. Screenwriter and pop culture commentator Vaibhav Vishal wrote in a column, '[Kader Khan] catered to the lowest common denominator without any apology. He was of the people, for the people, by the people – only louder, shriller, piercing. [He] brought the lowbrow out of its cultural closet.' Kader Khan applied his zany imagination to the screenplays and came out with crowd-favourite lines that critics panned. In *Himmatwala*, for example, the character he played spoke only in place names!

The third ace in the pack was the combination of composer Bappi Lahiri and lyricist Indeevar, whose inane lyrics ('*Mamma mia pom pom*') matched the former's heavily orchestrated music and dance beats. The dances were choregraphed by an invisible PT teacher in fields of dreams populated by yards of cloth (*Tohfa*), large clay pots (*Himmatwala*), large brass pots (*Tohfa* again), synthetic lotus ponds (*Mawaali*) or a jalopy (*Justice Chaudhury*).

Usually Sridevi and/or Jaya Prada were the female leads – almost always playing a shrew in the initial scenes before succumbing to Jeetendra's wigged charms, and matching him step for step in song sequences. Both went on to have thriving careers in Bollywood as well.

As family audiences moved away from theatres due to the video boom, the aggressive combination of song, dance, action and melodrama still drew people to cinemas and many of the films were massive money-spinners. *Himmatwala* and *Tohfa* were the top-grossers of 1983 and 1984 respectively. Both were directed by K. Raghavendra Rao, with whom Jeetendra eventually made 11 films.

Thirty years later, the biggest hit of 2011 – *The Dirty Picture* – was set in the world of 1980s South Indian films. It not only spoofed the biting-lips-heaving-bosoms-among-pots variety of songs visually, but also lifted the tune from a hit song in *Mawaali*. The film was produced by Ekta Kapoor – daughter of one Jeetendra.

Gangotri, Rishikesh, Benaras, Calcutta

Ram Teri Ganga Maili, 1985

Raj Kapoor was shooting for *Jis Desh Mein Ganga Behti Hai* in Calcutta when he heard the story. Legend goes that Totapuri Maharaj – a saint from Rishikesh – had come down to Calcutta, and met the famous Bengali mystic, Ramakrishna Paramahamsa, on the banks of Hooghly River – the name by which the Ganga is known before it enters the Bay of Bengal. Used to the pristine Ganga of Rishikesh, and pained by the filth flowing in the river at Calcutta, he told Ramakrishna, 'Ram, *teri Ganga kitni maili hai!*' To which Ramakrishna replied that the river is dirty only because it washes away human sin as it makes its way towards the sea. '*Ram teri Ganga maili ho gayi, paapiyon ke paap dhotey dhotey…*' was the title song and thematic message of Raj Kapoor's biggest hit, which he made a quarter of a century after he heard the story. To allude to the tale, the name of his hero was Naren (played by his son Rajiv Kapoor) after Ramakrishna's most famous disciple, Narendranath Dutta, aka Swami Vivekananda.

Ram Teri Ganga Maili opens in the hills of Uttarakhand, near the source of the Ganga. The heroine, Ganga, is as pristine and unspoilt as the river there, till she is promised marriage and impregnated by a city man from the end of the river. She leaves her village with her son, and tries to reach her husband – 'becoming dirty' as she travels down the path of the Ganga. Every major city in her journey causes misfortune to befall her. At Rishikesh, she is swindled. At Benares (now Varanasi), she is molested by a priest. By the time she reaches Calcutta, her 'fall' is complete as she is sold to a brothel. Eventually, she reaches Calcutta and is made to perform at her husband's wedding to another woman.

Director Raj Kapoor expressed the symbolism quite literally, and filmed the Ganga at its source, Gangotri. Over 60 years old at the time of shooting, he had to be carried in *dolis* up to the ice cave of Gaumukh above the Gangotri glacier at an altitude of nearly 4,100 metres. To portray the river as a woman, Raj Kapoor insisted on having 'somebody who had never been seen before and could not be identified with anything else.' Mandakini became that girl when she and her father came to Bombay from Meerut, gave a screen test and was selected from several other contenders. Raj Kapoor said she 'looked like Ganga and became Ganga'.

Ram Teri Ganga Maili was roundly criticized for its nudity. The most iconic image from the film is Mandakini under a waterfall, her nipples clearly visible under her flimsy saree. It is a wonder how it got past the conservative censor board of the time (that too, with a Universal rating)! But Raj Kapoor insisted that the nudity was symbolic of the river's purity. Which got exploited and spoilt by the sinners she encountered along the way.

Doordarshan

In Which Annie Gives It Those Ones, 1989

Before Arundhati Roy became a sensation as a Booker Prize–winning author, she and director Pradip Krishen (whom she later married) tried making an ambitious 26-part television series called *Bargad*. The show – based on India's freedom struggle – was researched and written over nearly two years before the production company pulled the plug. Roy and Krishen met with the then director-general of Doordarshan, Bhaskar Ghose, to figure out options to revive the show. Instead, Ghose offered them a chance to make a telefilm about people like themselves – young, urban and confused, with real quirks and tics. And thus was born a film – which writer Arundhati Roy called 'lunatic fringe cinema' – that became a cult favourite, despite being aired only once on television, that too late at night.

In Which Annie Gives It Those Ones is set in a fictional college of architecture, in the last few days before the final thesis presentation of the fifth-year students. It was Roy's writing debut and as real as she – an architecture student herself – could get. It captures the inane jokes, the pidgin lingo, the crazy dressing sense (think hats with sarees!) and the psychedelia of the era (May 1974, to be precise) in a way that's likely to leave people from later periods slack-jawed. The humour is laugh-out-loud funny and the film a crazy departure when compared to the Bollywood output of the times.

What is even crazier is the cast, or rather, the supporting cast. *Annie* marks the feature film debut of Shah Rukh Khan, who plays an effeminate 'senior' purveying gossip. Khan was an actor at Barry John's Theatre Action Group (TAG) and was tipped to play one of the leads in the film. He was already breaking into television (having shot for *Fauji*, that would give him his first taste of stardom), but the director found him 'already in the heroic mould' while the film was supposed to have no heroes. Apart from SRK, the hairy, grungy army of college students included Habib Faisal, Harsh Chhaya, Loveleen Mishra and Manoj Bajpayee. Among the other roles, there are Raghubir Yadav acting as a roadside Romeo and Himani Shivpuri as a rustic cabaret dancer in love with Annie.

Annie brilliantly epitomizes the schizophrenic nature of India's national television channel in the 1980s – it was simultaneously trying to be the government's mouthpiece and a birthplace of edgy content. Doordarshan of that era produced some path-breaking shows that created stars who made names for themselves in Bollywood, some of whom are around even today. One of the people behind this revolution at Doordarshan was Bhaskar Ghose, who had approved three telefilms. Two were by arthouse favourites – Aparna Sen and Goutam Ghose – while the third was *Annie*, which went on to win that year's Best Feature Film in English at the National Film Awards. Ironically, after he greenlit the film, Bhaskar Ghose was removed from his position for not toeing the government line. But his successor continued with the production and, in a decision not out of sync with the film's mood, he asked the makers to remove the words 'f***' and 'screw' from the script, but was okay with retaining 'screwed', 'shit' and 'balls'.

Interlaken

Switzerland, 1985–2012

'I know the area more than even the locals,' Yash Chopra said about Switzerland when describing his first foray into shooting there. During his most unsuccessful years (the mid-1980s), Yash Chopra directed the forgettable *Faasle*, but the film was an important milestone because it was the first time he shot in Switzerland. And went on to become synonymous with the country.

Yash Chopra was nowhere near being the first film-maker to shoot in Switzerland. Raj Kapoor had shot *Sangam* and Shakti Samanta had shot *An Evening in Paris* in the picturesque country, way back in the 1960s. It was not the first foreign location Chopra went to either, having picturized the song

'*Dekha ek khwab*' from *Silsila* in the tulip gardens of Keukenhof in the Netherlands. But with *Faasle,* something clicked, and Switzerland became a location he kept coming back to. Thanks to his fascination for the country and his cinematographer in his later years – Manmohan Singh –these lusciously shot romantic films in grand settings made him the 'King of Romance'.

Yash Chopra had used picturesque locations like Kashmir and Shimla as settings for his films, especially the early romantic dramas like *Daag, Kabhi Kabhie* and *Silsila.* His fascination for love stories in international locations probably stemmed from his three-month-long honeymoon, which was practically a world tour. When it became comparatively easier to shoot abroad in the 1980s and even more attractive – post India's economic liberalization – in the 1990s, he never looked away from Switzerland.

After *Faasle, Vijay* was also shot in Switzerland. And then *Chandni* came, which became the playbook for the Yash Chopra triptych – a woman in shimmering chiffons, the leads falling in love and an exotic location as the backdrop, aka Switzerland. In *Chandni,* Sridevi is promised a honeymoon in Switzerland (though the two heroes end up there, singing songs and becoming friends). Even without the plot requiring the crew to be in the country, Yash Chopra shot many a song in Switzerland,

and that started the process of creating the most attractive tourism brochures ever! Be it his own *Lamhe* and *Darr*, or Aditya Chopra's *Dilwale Dulhania Le Jayenge*, Switzerland was the go-to destination for Yash Raj Films. The venerable director wanted to shoot a token sequence in Switzerland for his last film *Jab Tak Hai Jaan* as well, but passed away before the final shoot.

After him, other film-makers also followed suit, and the net result was an exponential rise of Indian tourists to Switzerland – to the extent that there are Indian snack bars and restaurants at most important tourist spots in the country. And Swiss Tourism expressed their gratitude by naming him 'Ambassador of Interlaken' and even naming a train in Jungfrau Railway after him. A hotel has named their most luxurious suite after Yash Chopra, and Lake Lauenen is unofficially referred to as Lake Chopra. But the most affectionate tribute is probably the bronze statue of Yash Chopra and his camera, located near the city centre of Interlaken. As his wife, Pamela Chopra, put it at the unveiling ceremony, 'He did some of the best work of his life here.'

Kashmir

Roja, 1992

A newly married girl from rural Tamil Nadu moves to Kashmir with her husband, who is working on a government project. One day, her husband closes her eyes and leads her to a valley, and when she is allowed to open her eyes, she – and the audience – gasp in wonder at the snow-capped mountains and tall chinar trees. For at least one generation of audiences, *Roja* was the 'rebirth' of Kashmir in Hindi cinema.

Yash Chopra, the last of the great Kashmir fans, had last shot *Silsila* there before discovering Switzerland and making it his playground. Another old-time showman's – Raj Kapoor – dream project, *Henna*, had a part of the film located in Kashmir, but Pakistan was the major focus of the story. Due to increasing militancy in the Valley and the easing of foreign exchange norms, Bollywood had abandoned Kashmir for foreign locales, and audiences didn't seem to miss the picturesque mountain region through the 1980s. Mani Ratnam's acclaimed *Roja* (made in Tamil and dubbed in Hindi) was probably the first time that Kashmir's politics and terrain were integral to the story. Unlike the 1960s – when Kashmir first became popular – it wasn't just a pretty backdrop.

Roja's story is borrowed from Hindu mythology. It is the story of Savitri and Satyavan, where the husband is taken away by the Lord of Death (kidnapped by militants in the film), but the wife's devotion (obstinate badgering of security forces in the film) brings him back. Ratnam zeroed-in on Kashmir because the militancy provided a plausible backdrop for the kidnapping, but also for the novelty value: Most people didn't know much about Kashmir's situation at that time. And to make more people aware of what was happening, the film didn't paint the militants as dark, soulless murderers. With the addition of a Kashmiri girl – who plays the militant leader's sister – Ratnam said (in Baradwaj Rangan's *Conversations with Mani Ratnam*) that he made the militants 'a little real, a little more rooted… The militants could be a reflection of [the kidnapped engineer] on the other side'.

Roja started several trends. It was A.R. Rahman's debut film. It also kicked off Mani Ratnam's trilogy of movies that explored human relationships against the backdrop of Indian politics (the other two films being *Bombay* and *Dil Se*).

In the context of India's 'Heaven on Earth', *Roja* came at a time when the militancy had worsened and the exodus of Kashmiri Hindus had happened just a couple of years ago. The movie revealed Kashmir as a stunningly beautiful place ravaged by a terrible political situation, which threw up unlikely heroes and villains. From the early 2000s, there have been a flurry of films on Kashmir. Some have used it simply as a gorgeous locale, while others have explored the theme of terrorism – the treatments ranging from realistic to over-the-top.

And, in a matter of irony typical to the dream factory, *Roja* was not shot in Kashmir at all! Due to the volatile situation on the ground, most of the breath-taking sequences around snowy mountains were filmed around Manali in Himachal Pradesh. But as Mani Ratman explained the title: '[*Roja*] represented Kashmir because the rose is something beautiful but with thorns.'

The poster of *Mission Kashmir* showed a shikara exploding on Dal Lake, an apt symbol of a heaven on earth torn asunder by terrorism.

Image courtesy of Vinod Chopra Films

Ooty

1990s

Bollywood has the strangest ways of making hits. Film-maker Indra Kumar was a certified hitmaker of the 1990s. He resurrected Aamir Khan's career (*Dil*), boosted Anil Kapoor's (*Beta*), (re)launched Sanjay Kapoor's (*Raja*) and made a multi-starrer superhit (*Ishq*). Apparently, the lucky charm binding all of these films was a tree in Ooty around which he had to shoot at least one scene. It was only when he reached Ooty for this fifth film – *Mann* – that he realized the tree had been cut down! *Mann* was a resounding flop, and it took Indra Kumar several years to get his mojo back.

Nearly 20 years before *Mann*, Monty Oberoi had visions of his previous birth in *Karz* and was advised to recuperate in

Ooty – coincidentally, the exact location of his previous birth. Subhash Ghai wrote the first draft of *Karz* in Ooty, and decided to locate the film there.[7] The shoot obviously held many fond memories for the cast because Rishi Kapoor went back to the ballroom of Fernhills Royal Palace Hotel decades later, and reminisced about shooting there. As Southern film-makers reached Bollywood and Bollywood stars reached the South, Ooty became a preferred shooting destination – its hilly locales replacing Kashmir and Shimla in the 1980s. Between *Sadma* and *Hum*, Ooty had reached mainstream Bollywood by the end of the 1980s.

But this was nothing compared to the 1990s. An avalanche of films with the best stars moved Ooty-wards and the locations became more familiar than studio sets. Madhuri Dixit once said that 95 per cent of her films were shot in Ooty, and the number for Juhi Chawla would have been in the same range. However, the strongest association of Ooty was with a seemingly fading star.

Mithun Chakraborty – his film career in a downward spiral – moved lock, stock and barrel to Ooty and started his career

---

7. Probably the first Hindi film to be shot in Ooty was *Sangam*, whose '*O mehbooba*' song was picturized on Ooty Lake, which looked absolutely unspoiled in the scenes.

as a hotelier there. And as the country's most business-friendly movie star. He opened Hotel Monarch in Ooty and offered an all-inclusive package to film-makers – shoot in Ooty with Mithun, stay at his hotel and get bulk dates to complete the film on time. Compared to the several months (if not years) that took a Bollywood film of the 1990s to be made, the Mithun's Dream Factory (yes, that was the name of the studio!) ensured a full film – from scripting to release – fully ready in a couple of months. Ooty was the location for more than a hundred Mithun films in the decade, which meant almost every month for 10 years had a Mithun release. These films were made on shoestring budgets, used almost the same cast, looked identical because of the same location, but ran so well in the smaller towns of India that it earned him the title of 'Bollywood's B-Grade King'. Did I say that Bollywood has the strangest way of making hits?

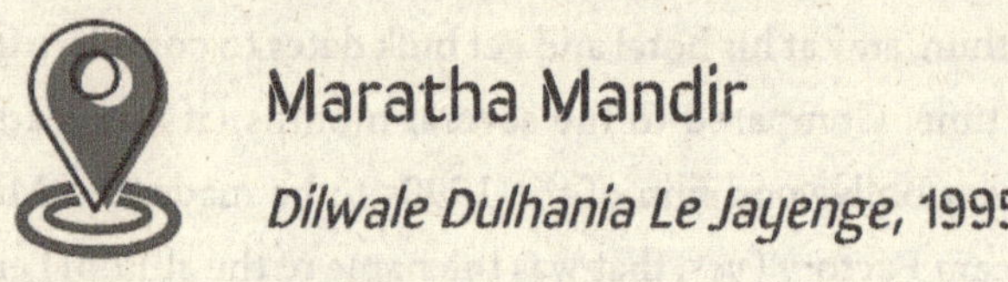

Maratha Mandir

Dilwale Dulhania Le Jayenge, 1995

When *Mughal-e-Azam* released on 5 August 1960, it created a grand spectacle in one of the newer and grander theatres of Bombay – Maratha Mandir. A massive 40-feet cut-out of Prithviraj Kapoor as Emperor Akbar dominated the outer façade, while the other two stars – Dilip Kumar and Madhubala – along with the film's reels, arrived on elephants, making the premiere as grand as the film itself. This was in line with the unprecedented buzz around the movie, when 1 lakh people landed up outside the theatre on the opening of advance bookings. And the excitement didn't seem to diminish at all, because the film ran to near capacity at Maratha Mandir for three years.

Maratha Mandir – a 1,112-seater theatre – opened on 16 October 1958, and the first film that played there was *Sadhna* starring Sunil Dutt and Vyjayanthimala. The mega-success of *Mughal-e-Azam* and the subsequent craze around it made it one of the most prestigious theatres in Bombay. However, it was a film that released in 1995 that established the theatre in the national consciousness. *Dilwale Dulhania Le Jayenge* from Yash Raj Films and the directorial debut of Yash Chopra's son, Aditya, was always supposed to be a money-spinner, but nobody could have imagined how much it would make. *DDLJ* released on 19 October 1995 in Maratha Mandir and kept running. And running. And running. And running.

There are many theories of why this happened. One goes that due to its proximity to Mumbai Central station, outstation visitors, transit travellers and railway staff often come down to Maratha Mandir to watch the film to pass time and catch a piece of history. Another goes that due to the low prices of the tickets (₹20 to ₹30), casual moviegoers and couples looking for some privacy find this a peaceful haven to retire in for three hours. But nothing really explains the 1,300+ weeks of the film running.

Over the years, the run has seen its share of drama. In 2011, during a strike of single-screen theatres in Mumbai, the managing director of Maratha Mandir – Manoj Desai – shifted the shows to the multiplex – G7 in Bandra – he owned to ensure that the film's run remained unbroken. In 2015, after 20 years and 1,000+ weeks, the film was taken off screen citing low demand. But fans of *DDLJ* vociferously demanded its continuation. Seeing the popular demand, Yash Raj Films intervened and it is said a financial package was worked out to ensure the film continues to run at Maratha Mandir.

Even now, you can log on to online ticket booking apps and buy a ticket for *DDLJ*, which is still likely to be running at 50 per cent capacity in this landmark theatre on weekends. Occasionally, crazy things happen. Like the time a man came to Maratha Mandir and booked all the seats – just so he and his girlfriend could watch the movie alone. And he probably proposed to her after the film. *Bade bade theatres mein aisi chhoti chhoti baatein hoti reheti hai.*

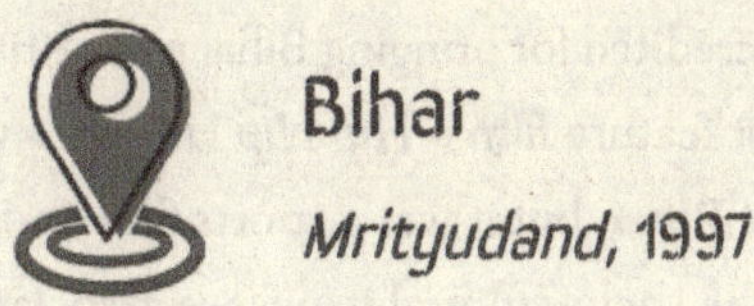

Bihar has a terrible reputation. Casteism. Feudalism. Patriarchy. The inherent violence of all three in an environment of lawlessness. Prakash Jha – being from the state – knew this well, but it was driven home when he heard of a particularly brutal incident. A village panchayat head had ordered a few men to rape a woman because she didn't want to marry within her community. This was one of the triggers for him writing *Mrityudand*.

Set in a typical village in Bihar, *Mrityudand* is the story of three women fighting against centuries of oppression. The story had been explored many times, especially in parallel cinema. Where *Mrityudand* differed was the treatment, exemplified by the leading lady. Superstar Madhuri Dixit played Ketki, an educated woman, who marries into a conservative rural household and rebels against the exploitation she faces.

Prakash Jha can be credited for bringing Bihar as a setting into Hindi cinema. His first feature film – *Hip Hip Hurray* – was set in Ranchi, then part of Bihar, but it was a sports film and didn't particularly focus on the socio-cultural issues we associate with Bihar. His second film, *Damul*, was about bonded labour and the consequent migration of people from Bihar. It was hard-hitting and gritty and won the National Award for Best Film, but didn't get a major theatrical release. After working on documentaries and TV shows, Jha returned to Bihar with *Mrityudand* 12 years later. Critics found the film brave and progressive, and it was declared the sleeper hit of the year.

With *Mrityudand*, the template for the 'Bihar film' was set. The next movie to be noticed was E. Niwas's *Shool*, in which Manoj Bajpayee took up arms against a Bihari politician, Bachchu Yadav (Sayaji Shinde). The villain was a caricature of the typical Bihari politician, and once again portrayed a stereotype that would be revisited time and again. Prakash Jha himself made *Gangaajal*, *Apaharan* and *Jai Gangaajal* that were set in Bihar and made liberal use of the template he himself had created. All these films took real incidents like the Bhagalpur blindings and Bihar's kidnapping industry to build a believable backdrop, and used top stars to draw in the crowds. Over the years, the 'Bihar film' has sometimes become more granular and sometimes grander. A film like *Anaarkali of Aarah* explores the life of a small-time erotic folk dancer. While *Half Girlfriend* shows us the challenges Bihar's youth face, hamstrung by the lack of opportunities and the inability to speak English. But the biggest Bihar film, *Gangs of Wasseypur* – strictly speaking – is set in present-day Jharkhand. The chronology of the film places it mostly in united Bihar and, more importantly, the mood of the film is uniquely Bihari. At the premiere of the film in Cannes, the cast and crew appeared wearing *gamchhas* to showcase the flavour of the film. The humble Bihari had finally hit big time.

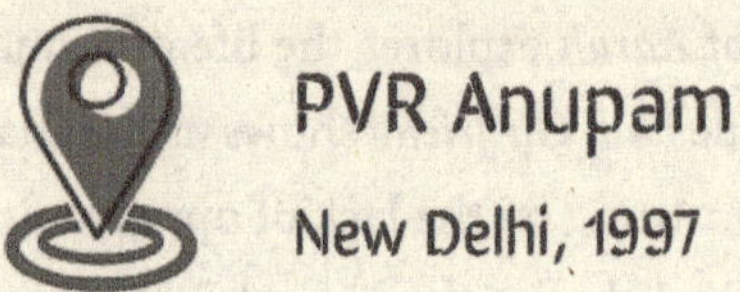

PVR Anupam

New Delhi, 1997

'You mean that at this price I can watch movies at all four theatres, right?' asked one incredulous fellow at the ticket counter of India's first multiplex. This was the opening week, and he had just heard that a single ticket cost ₹75. PVR Anupam had opened as 'Anupam 4' to drive home the message that audiences could now watch four films under one roof. And their ticket price was nearly triple the going rate of ₹25–30 then. No wonder people thought that a single ticket entitled them to watch shows in all four theatres.

Ajay and Sanjeev Bijli were from a family that ran a transport business and owned one theatre in South Delhi – it was named Priya. They remodelled Priya with new projection and Dolby sound systems, apart from plush seating, better carpets and air-conditioning. Priya's footfall picked up as a top destination for Hollywood films in Delhi. After their father passed away, and a fire majorly affected their transport business, they entered a joint venture with Australia's Village Roadshow Limited to open a multiplex in India. Thus was born Priya Village Roadshow, which became famous as PVR – the company that amped up both the cinema-going experience and ticket prices in India.

While multiplexes face a lot of flak for their higher ticket prices, it is undeniable that they made a massive difference in the way India watches movies. It led to the creation of the 'multiplex crowd' – an urban and hip audience, who didn't mind paying high ticket prices for a movie they identified with, in an ambience that made them feel at home. This led to a tectonic change in the way movies were made in India. From pan-India mass entertainers – with a mix of action, romance, comedy, music and melodrama – we moved into a genre of movies that were still entertaining, but didn't insist on having every single masala ingredient in excessive quantities. In the few years after PVR opened in Delhi, multiplex chains popped up in every metro city and movies changed forever. Films like *Dil Chahta Hai* started becoming top grossers because the Bollywood genre of 'film for the classes' could make several times the revenue per screen compared to the 'film for the masses'. The journey that started in South Delhi's Saket became India's largest multiplex chain and a prime mover in film exhibition. The last two decades have seen great theatre experiences, as well as a longing for the old single-screen, with their whirring fans and oily samosas.

The split between single-screen and multiplex audiences is best brought out by two male stars shooting for Zoya Akhtar's *Dil Dhadakne Do*. Anil Kapoor and Ranveer Singh developed a code for subtle ('multi') and over-the-top acting ('single'). 'Zoya *bol rahi hai* multi *karo, lekin main soch raha hoon thoda* single *karoon*' was how they chose to describe the difference in audience tastes due to the 3x differential in ticket prices! PVR – literally and metaphorically – redefined the way film-makers saw their audiences.

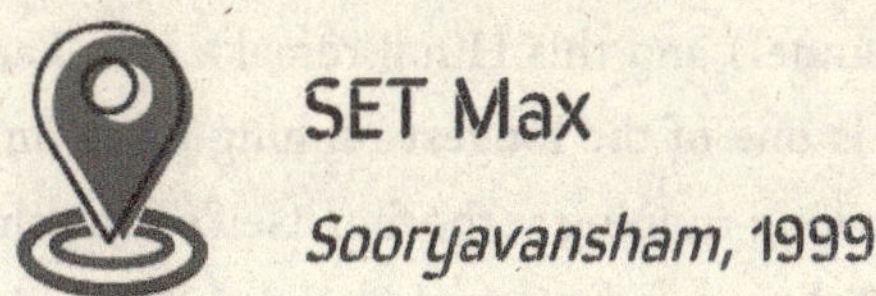

SET Max

Sooryavansham, 1999

Two of the biggest hits of 2017 – *Baahubali 2: The Conclusion* and *Golmaal Again* – were the top-rated films in the weeks (of October 2017 and February 2018, respectively) they premiered on television. And quite expectedly so. What was unexpected was that in both weeks there was one common title among the five most-watched films on television in the country – the 1999 Amitabh Bachchan–starrer *Sooryavansham*. The movie has often been called the 'most-watched film on Indian television' by its stars. Since BARC (India's television rating agency) doesn't release lifetime data, it is difficult to verify this claim, but it doesn't seem wrong. After all, *Sooryavansham* was among the most-watched films on television in (at least) 2017, 2018 and 2019.

The 'love story' between SET Max (Sony network's Hindi movie channel) and this Hindi remake of a Tamil hit (*Suryavamsam*) is one of the longest-running jokes on social media, but not as long-running as the film itself on the channel! For starters, SET Max was launched in July 1999, which was just a couple of months after the film released. It is said that the fledgling channel was buying rights for recently released films, and this movie – which flopped on release – was going for cheap. It is also said that SET Max bought the television rights for the film for 100 years. But this still doesn't explain the frequency of the airings. Business heads from the channel have spoken about television viewing as a community activity and that films which do well on television are usually social dramas or comedies, without any explicit content or unduly dark themes. *Sooryavansham* – the story of a dynamic patriarch's wastrel son eventually coming good – ticks off all these boxes.

The plot points were familiar to start off with, and with repeated viewings, they have become cornerstones of the meme world. Thakur Bhanu Pratap Singh (Amitabh Bachchan) and his family's ill-treatment of his son Heera (also Amitabh Bachchan) is portrayed in the typical heavy-handed manner that now seems out of place with an audience exposed to more mature cinema. The son's determined but polite rise to success as an entrepreneur and eventual reconciliation with his father – despite the villainous machinations of the family's enemies – is also reminiscent of the Bollywood of yore. All the set pieces that are so popular on television routinely get mocked on social media through hilarious memes. If there was any doubt about the existence of two Indias, the success of *Sooryavansham* on television and on social media quite literally proves it.

And SET Max is in on this. On 27 May 2018, the first IPL final took place outside of the Sony network. (Sony had lost its IPL rights to the Star network earlier that year.) And, either as a nod to their true fans or as a troll of epic proportions, SET Max aired *Sooryavansham* that night. #HeeraThakurFTW

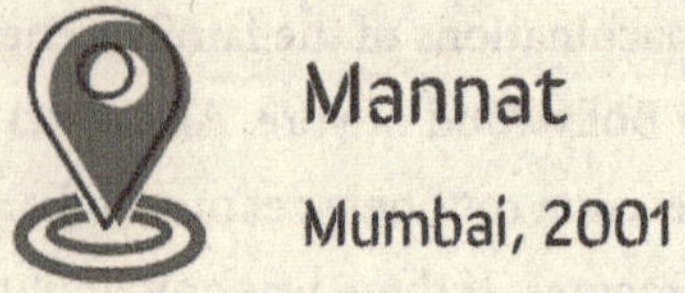

Mannat

Mumbai, 2001

Kekoo Gandhy was an art collector and gallery owner, who ran the business of manufacturing frames, and showcased works of then-young artists like M.F. Husain, S.H. Raza, Tyeb Mehta and the like. He lived in a building called Kekee Manzil in Bandra, which was something like the nerve centre for India's art scene in the 1960s and 1970s. One day, in the 1990s, he came home and found a huge trench dug outside his house, presumably to set up the phone connection of his new neighbour. That neighbour – an upcoming film star – came to meet him and apologized for the inconvenience caused. Gandhy was mollified, and became friends with Shah Rukh Khan.

One of Gandhy's relatives owned a bungalow called Villa Vienna, at a fantastic location in Bandra, which offered a view of the sea. The newly minted star Shah Rukh felt he didn't want to live in Mumbai's boxy apartments, and wanted a bungalow like a true Dilliwala. He connected with Nariman Dubash, the owner of the villa, and convinced him to sell the property for ₹13.32 crore – an astronomical amount then.

The bungalow was a designated heritage structure, and was in a state of disrepair. As soon as Shah Rukh bought it and started renovation, controversies emerged about the extent of change being brought about and if it was permissible – legally and morally. SRK deftly negotiated through that maze of controversy to build the six-storeyed house that's probably Mumbai's best-known address now, and a piece of heaven on earth. Maybe that's why he initially considered calling it 'Jannat'. The mammoth effort that went into it can be seen even in casual social media exchanges. A Twitter user once asked Shah Rukh, 'Sir, *Mannat pe ek* room rent *pe chahiye. Kitne ka padega?*' and SRK replied, '*30 saal ki mehnat mein padega.*'

After Amitabh Bachchan's Prateeksha and Jalsa, Mannat is the only other star property that's become a Mumbai landmark. To achieve this status, a home must belong to a legendary star (SRK – check), look imposing (Greco-Roman façade – check), have an iconic location (Bandra Bandstand – check) and be conducive to large gatherings (double check). Mannat is all this and more, a place where the faithful congregate to get a glimpse of their god. While it still doesn't have the Sunday darshan à la Bachchan, the crazed crowds have been documented for posterity in international shows like *My Next Guest Needs No Introduction with David Letterman* and movies like *Fan.*

Before *Fan* and even before the sprawling bungalow became SRK's home, it had already been used as a shooting location for several films. It had been Madhuri Dixit's house in *Tezaab*. It had been Kader Khan's house-cum-durbar in *Angaar*. But the most interesting one is when a part of it was shown for a split second in a song. The song was '*Bas itna sa khwab hai*' from the film *Yes Boss* starring one Shah Rukh Khan. That's the real meaning of Mannat – where your dreams come true.

Goa

Dil Chahta Hai, 2001

An elderly couple in an ad for Vodafone (in 2017) went around asking locals in Goa for directions to the '*Dil Chahta Hai* fort' till the mobile connection (and Google Maps) came to their rescue. A year earlier, Google itself had launched an ad in which a film-crazy father–son duo searched for the same location as a part of their sightseeing adventures. A decade-and-a-half after the film released, this is not a bad indicator of the craze it started – not just for Chapora Fort (yes, that's its actual name) but for Goa in general.

Farhan Akhtar's directorial debut changed the way Hindi film audiences looked at three things – friendships, rich people and Goa. And, in a way, the last one was how the first two happened.

While interning at an ad film company, Farhan Akhtar started writing the script of *Dil Chahta Hai* as vignettes of the time he had spent in Goa with his friends. And then merged those 'diaries' with a story idea he got from a childhood friend.

In *Dil Chahta Hai,* the filmi vows of undying friendship got replaced by silly pranks. Sacrifices for friends gave way to petty squabbles. And the sentimental friendship song was replaced by a simple wish – may the good times never end ('*Dil chahta hai, kabhi na beete yeh chamkeele din*'). It was a 'buddy film', in which you could find yourself and your friends in Akash, Sid and Sameer. And Goa was the perfect place to showcase this friendship – a place you can just retire to and recharge yourself, drinking beer with your friends and thinking of girls.

It was the first mainstream Hindi film to show 'real rich' and not 'filmi rich'. The rich didn't stay in large mansions with sweeping staircases, nor did they go off to Switzerland just to sing a song. *Dil Chahta Hai* stripped the 'rich brat' tag from rich brats and presented them as regular guys with love problems, petty squabbles and bad jokes. And when they zipped off to Goa at a moment's notice – in a Mercedes convertible, no less – it seemed like something we all should do. (Yeah, but maybe without the convertible.) As the trio of friends – Aamir Khan, Akshaye Khanna and Saif Ali Khan – sat on the wall of Chapora

Fort and contemplated returning to this favourite holiday destination every year as a group, they were setting friendship goals for us as well.

And *Dil Chahta Hai* presented the grandest tourism video for the state. Cinematographer Ravi Chandran shot in natural light and with unobtrusive camera angles to make the Goa sequence absolutely real, seen through the eyes of friends. For example, the drive to Goa was shot from morning to evening because that's the time spent on a real trip. Only a small part of *Dil Chahta Hai* was set in Goa, but the three friends managed to squeeze in paragliding, massages, eating at shacks, fishing, boat cruises and even a love affair in that short burst. Both as holiday destination and a shooting location, Goa's popularity zoomed after *Dil Chahta Hai*. More Hindi films were set in Goa in the last 20 years than in the previous 80. Welcome to Goa, Singham!

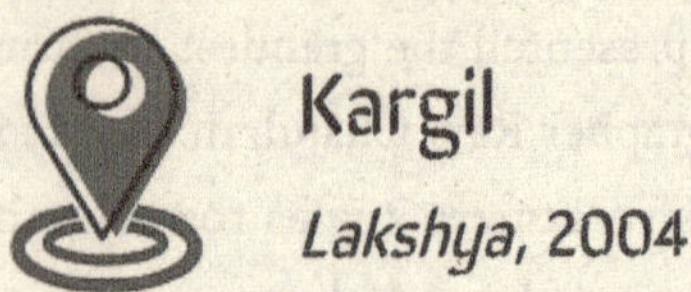

Kargil

Lakshya, 2004

Javed Akhtar had gone to Kargil to commemorate Vijay Diwas. He was told by a senior army officer there that the armed forces received a lot of praise and accolades for their operations, but the number of people enrolling in the army was going down every year. The officer wondered if this could be addressed. Javed Akhtar promised to write a film which would address this problem. And he wrote the script that would become *Lakshya.*

Despite winning three wars against Pakistan (before Kargil), India doesn't have a tradition of war movies. Such movies were few and far in between, and the one considered the best in the genre was *Haqeeqat* – based on the 1962 Chinese aggression, which we had lost. One of the most successful commercially was *Border*, based on a stand of immense courage during the 1971 Pakistan war. *Lakshya* was not the first film on the Kargil war. J.P. Dutta's *L.O.C. Kargil* released before that, boasting of a star cast that included pretty much all of Bollywood and a running length that broke records. Unfortunately, it broke no box-office records.

After his father started writing the script, Farhan got excited enough by the theme to take it on himself. But he was sure he didn't want to make an overblown war movie. The result was a beautiful coming-of-age film about a drifter (Hrithik Roshan) finally finding his aim in life – in the icy heights of Kargil – as a young army officer. About the shoot, Farhan says, 'I never worked harder than when I worked on that film.' The hostile terrain of Kargil was replicated in Ladakh, with active support from the Indian army. The shoot went on for five months, which included physically and technically gruelling battle scenes – sometimes shot very late at night. During the shoot, Farhan's weight dropped to 58 kilos and the result seemed worth his while.

The box office didn't agree, however, and *Lakshya* – despite getting good reviews – did only average business. Farhan Akhtar went into depression and, by his own admission, it took him nearly a year to come out of it.

In 2017, Farhan Akhtar was in Dehradun for a concert, and visited the Indian Military Academy (IMA) there. It was the first time he was visiting the place after the shooting of *Lakshya*. He was taken around the campus and then brought to the hall with all the cadets at the academy – more than a thousand of them. The senior officer asked the large group, 'How many of you decided to join the army because of the film *Lakshya*?' And 70 per cent of the hands went up.

Lakshya had become a success beyond the confines of the box-office.

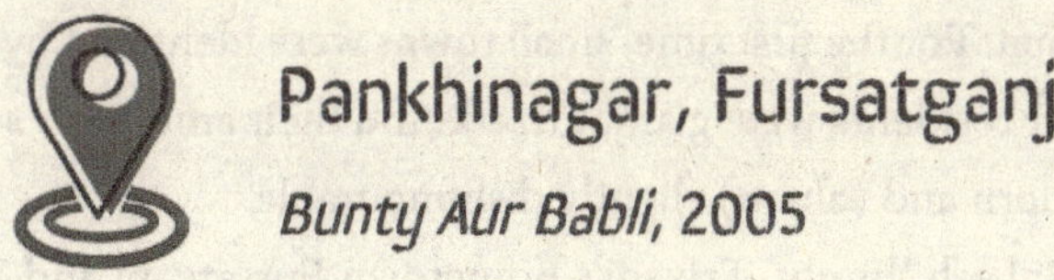

The title credits of *Bunty Aur Babli* gives us a lay of the film's land. There are signposts of various cities of Uttar Pradesh and Uttarakhand – Lucknow, Agra, Rishikesh, Banda, Bulandshahr, Mirzapur. Curiously, the milestones of several of them show 420 kms – indicating the section of the Indian Penal Code Raj Kapoor made famous nearly six decades previously. *Shree 420*'s hero was also a small-town boy and the city of Bombay corrupted him. In *Bunty Aur Babli*, the Bonnie and Clyde of Uttar Pradesh didn't have to go all the way to Mumbai to go rogue. They started their criminal careers right in the Hindi heartland, and the small towns were no longer the anonymous idylls of yore. For ages, Hindi cinema has used the simplistic 'big city = bad and village = innocent' equation. Within the village, the rich people – zamindars and moneylenders – were evil and the virtuous lived in poverty. *Bunty Aur Babli* changed all that. For the first time, small towns were identified by name. Their residents were glamourized. And their ambitions seemed modern and (ahem) slightly dishonourable.

Rakesh 'Bunty' Trivedi's hometown Fursatganj and Vimmi 'Babli' Saluja's Pankhinagar may sound fictitious to the city slicker, but real areas exist by those names. And every con the duo perpetrate are set in real towns, mostly linked to a major landmark. Their first swindle is in Kanpur, which they celebrate by having chaat in the city's famous 'Thaggu ke Laddu'. The legendary sweet shop's tagline '*Aisa koi sagaa nahin, jisko (humne) thagaa nahin*' found its way into the title song's lyrics by Gulzar. After that, Bunty and Babli assume their criminal alter egos on a bus and embark on an adventure that takes them to Kanpur, Lakshman Jhoola, Bulandshahr, Mussoorie, Bareilly, Agra and, finally, Delhi.

Pankhinagar and Fursatganj were representative of every small town in North India, which seem too slow and empty for the ambitious. '*Chhote chhote shehron se, khaali bhor dopehron se, hum toh jhola uthake chalein*' is the opening song in which the two lead characters give their statements of purpose – to become rich and famous, by hook or by crook. Their cons are carefully constructed to establish them as Robin Hoods, glossing over the misdemeanours and showing them as glamourous role models instead. *Bunty Aur Babli* did become the shorthand name for couple-criminals, and there still seems to be a lot of them as seen in newspaper reports about their heists. No one can really tell how many were inspired by the film. What the movie did inspire though was fashion. Abhishek Bachchan wearing his watch over a wristband, and Rani Mukerji's short kurtis and Patiala salwars became quite the rage.

Writer Jaideep Sahni, a first-rate chronicler of the middle-class, creates a fine balance between the real ambitions that exist in the small towns of India and the filmi fulfilments of these. *Bunty Aur Babli* were the superhero avatars of millions of commoners, whose stories started becoming the focus of Bollywood. The North Indian small town is now a staple location for Hindi films. And *Bunty Aur Babli* brought it to us first.

Passionforcinema.com

World Wide Web, 2006–2011

'Leaving in two hours for Jaipur to finally complete *Gulaal*. The film I have been trying to do for last six years,' started the blog post on 22 June 2008 – written by Anurag Kashyap before he became Anurag Kashyap. It explained in detail how *Gulaal* was developed and the struggles he faced to make it. The chaotic site on which this blog was written was called passionforcinema.com (PFC). It had become India's most passionate movies site, if not the most popular one. If 'engagement' is the metric website owners go for, PFC was right up there on top with the very best.

The site was started by Pankaj Sikka (pen name: Oz) and his friends (including today's familiar names like Vasan Bala, Somen

Mishra and Kartik Krishnan). Anurag Kashyap was one of the prime movers behind it – he started blogging on the website after seeing the passionate fan following he had on the site. The early members of PFC often landed up at his home, managing to see first cuts of *Dev D* and *Ugly*. Along with him, the who's who of contemporary Indian cinema were present on PFC. Abhay Deol, Dibakar Banerjee, Hansal Mehta, Sudhir Mishra, Revathy and Sujoy Ghosh were among the others who contributed as guest bloggers. Film-maker Onir wrote a post on making films of his choice in an industry averse to taking risks. Onir went on to raise money through crowdfunding for his film *I Am*, and that blog post on PFC was one of the early markers of his initiative.

That film-makers found the site interesting enough to engage with fans was only one aspect of PFC. It was also a talent-discovery platform. On a blog post about the shooting of *No Smoking* by Anurag Kashyap, Varun Grover wrote a poem as a comment – pitching it as a song for the film. Kashyap liked it enough to call Grover home. It eventually led to Grover writing lyrics for *That Girl in Yellow Boots* and then *Gangs of Wasseypur*. Director of *Masaan*, Neeraj Ghaywan, was a corporate executive, writing passionate posts on topics as diverse as *Kaminey*, Federico Fellini and Bollywood clichés on PFC before quitting his job and landing up in Mumbai.

From an obituary for Joginder to a review of *Drona,* from an appreciation of filmi villains to a piece on *Indiana Jones,* PFC's range was manna from heaven for the voracious movie fan. Many posts had wonky grammar, poor syntax and non-existent formatting. It is obvious they were written in breathless bursts, maybe late at night or during a frustrating day at the office. Many were angry (or sarcastic) rejoinders to earlier posts. PFC's annual contests for reviews and short films received massive response. It was truly fuelled by passion for cinema and came to be seen as a platform for alternate cinema.

Eventually PFC was shut down in April 2011 because of a rumoured fallout between Sikka and his friends about the future of PFC. The stated reason – in an emotional last post – was the organizers' lack of time to maintain such a site and a hope to have started a discussion about all kinds of cinema. Their range may have been replicated by a bunch of other sites. But the passion remains unmatched.

India Gate

Rang De Basanti, 2006

Director Rakeysh Omprakash Mehra and writer Kamlesh Pandey were shooting a documentary in Gujarat when they started exchanging stories of India's legendary freedom fighters – Bhagat Singh, Chandrasekhar Azad, Shivaram Rajguru, Ashfaqullah Khan and Ramprasad Bismil. They wrote a script on these heroes, but when they did some market research, the youth of the 21st century just couldn't identify with it. The script was then reworked into a modern-day protest about faulty fighter planes and the transformation of cynical youngsters into fighters for a different kind of freedom. And their battleground was India's most famous war memorial – India Gate.

Delhi, as seen in Hindi cinema, had mostly been about historical monuments and sprawling central vistas – which were primarily used for displaying romantic feelings or patriotic fervour. *Rang De Basanti* did their bit for Delhi (and Punjab and Rajasthan) Tourism, but used India Gate for a radically different purpose: As the venue of politically charged protests.

In the film, the government shifts the blame from itself (about sub-standard spares for MiG fighter planes) to a competent pilot, who sacrificed his life when his flight crashed. His friends start a peaceful candlelight vigil at India Gate which is met with brutal government action, leaving them battered and beaten. The film hurtles towards a devastating climax and ends with visuals of the youth from across the country promising to spread the fires of protests that these youngsters had kindled. This, however, didn't remain merely a filmi climax.

Rang De Basanti released on Republic Day of 2006. Three weeks later, a Delhi trial court acquitted all the accused in the Jessica Lal murder case for lack of evidence. The youth of Delhi took the idea from *Rang De Basanti* and started candlelight vigils at India Gate. In turn, the film on the Jessica Lal protests – *No One Killed Jessica* – shows a young girl coming out of a theatre playing *Rang De Basanti* and messaging her friends to congregate at India Gate to demand justice.

In the immediate aftermath of *Rang De Basanti,* at least three high profile cases – the Jessica Lal, Nitish Katara and Priyadarshini Mattoo cases – were reopened or examined with renewed diligence. This happened after a huge public outcry, much of which was expressed through massive vigils at India Gate. The power of silent protest at India's most well-known war memorial meant something as the accused in all three cases were found guilty in subsequent trials. This 'RDB Effect' was quite unprecedented – that a film would be directly credited for a public uprising.

However, in 2012, another peaceful protest near India Gate – demanding justice for a victim of gangrape in Delhi – was met with police lathis and water cannons, reminiscent of *Rang De Basanti*'s tragic end. But the youth of India refused to be defeated. They had found a place where they wanted to be seen and demanded to be heard.

New Khosla Kunj

Khosla Ka Ghosla!, 2006

'*Yahan peshaab karna mana hai,*' read the roughly painted sign on the newly constructed wall. The wall was around a plot of land (30/32 New Sapna Vihar) that Kamal Kishore Khosla had purchased from Vijender of World Famous Properties. The initial bemusement ('*Kamaal hai, ji, yahan peshaab thode hi karne aaye hain hum?*') gives way to horror when the Khosla family realizes that their plot of land has been illegally occupied by a landshark.

Scriptwriter Jaideep Sahni had faced this experience in his extended family, when an uncle's plot – one which they had invested their life's savings into – had been taken over by a landshark, who built a wall around it. Their story didn't have a happy ending, but Jaideep decided to convert this episode into a rollicking and rib-tickling but extremely real script. Ad-film-maker Dibakar Banerjee came on board for his directorial debut, and brought his own perspectives of being a Bengali in Delhi's Punjabi-dominated Karol Bagh. They started collaborating around 2003, but the film ran into rough weather, taking nearly two years to make. However, the subject hit bullseye because that was the time of a real-estate boom in Delhi NCR and many a shady deal was brokered. Along with the topicality was the freshness of flavour, reminiscent of Hrishikesh Mukherjee's middle-of-the-road cinema. A National Award for the Best Hindi Feature Film followed, along with moderate financial success on the back of extremely positive word of mouth. The writing of the film was masterful, creating several lines that became cult favourites. Like that ultimate query to test someone's position in the pecking order: '*Aap* broker *hain ya* party?'

The writer–director duo counted among its influences films like *Chashme Buddoor* and some deep research in the milieu of the film. The assistants on the film secretly recorded their conversations with several property dealers in Delhi, tapes of which were shared with Boman Irani to help him get into character. The Bombay-born Parsi internalized those conversations to become the wheeling-dealing Kishan Khurana.

Anupam Kher – a childhood favourite of the writer and director – was an easier sell. He loved the script and agreed to play the role of the retired middle-class Delhiite, who almost loses his life's savings to a devious villain and a corrupt system.

The location of New Sapna Vihar was realistically placed in the barren extremities of the NCR, where middle-class families had invested their life's savings to bring about Delhi's fabled real-estate boom. They paid through their nose to move to the seemingly posher locales, only to hear a jealous neighbour exclaim, '*Arre, Khosla sahab, aap bhi* South Delhi *wale ban gaye?*'

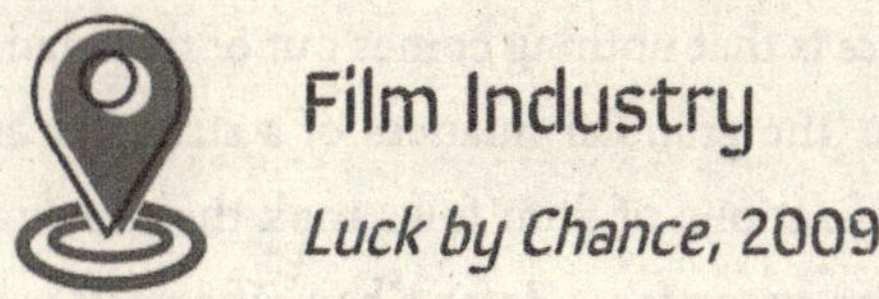

Film Industry

Luck by Chance, 2009

Zoya Akhtar grew up in a home which had a movie projector in it. She remembers her mother getting reels of films from theatre owners and projecting them on a wall. She specifically remembers watching *The Godfather* this way. After each movie, her parents' friends would sit around and discuss the script, the camera movements, the acting and everything else about the film. Zoya is a child of the film industry and possibly the best person to pay tribute to it.

Luck by Chance is as much an affectionate tribute to the Hindi film industry as it is a sharp critique of its ways. It is the story of a hustler, Vikram Jai Singh (Farhan Akhtar) from Delhi, who arrives in Mumbai to make it big. He falls in love with a junior artiste, Sona Mishra (Konkona Sen Sharma), who is trying to become a heroine. They start growing apart when he lands a big-budget film and his career becomes his priority. The beauty of *Luck by Chance* is that nothing comes out of this inadequate plot description. The granular nuances of a struggler and the minute characterizations of filmi folks took the movie to just another level. The superstar – Zafar Khan. The yesteryear star – Neena Walia. The star daughter – Nikki Walia. The veteran producer – Romy Rolly. The sidey producer – Satish Chaudhary. The producer's brother – Ranjit Rolly. The producer's wife – Minty Rolly. The acting coach – Nand Kishore. Every single star cameo, from Karan Johar to Mac Mohan, from Anurag Kashyap to Kareena Kapoor. In terms of memorable supporting characters, *Luck by Chance* probably rivals *Sholay*. With whom it shares a writer.

Zoya Akhtar wrote the story and screenplay of *Luck by Chance*, while her father, the legendary Javed Akhtar, wrote its dialogues. Zoya says Javed's lifetime in the film industry and his wicked sense of humour brought out many facets of each character. Where *Luck by Chance* diverges from other films on the industry is that it doesn't wear rose-tinted glasses. The brutal selfishness of stars. The casual nepotism. The implicit exploitation of the smaller fry. Stardom changing the equation between friends. Bollywood trying to corporatize, in a bumbling copycat way. *Luck by Chance* goes through all these – sometimes tongue firmly in cheek, and sometimes with an iron fist, hidden under a velvet glove.

The Hindi film industry is accused of being too formulaic. But *Luck by Chance*'s story is about the gumption of newcomers who took on the formula, and dared to do films no star would do. From Amitabh Bachchan doing *Zanjeer* to Shah Rukh Khan doing *Baazigar* to Vikram Jai Singh doing *Dil Ki Aag*, the strugglers have prevailed. Without money, family connections or conventional good looks, they perpetuated the magic of Bollywood by rising to the top. Aided by their hunger. Their talent. And a little bit of luck.

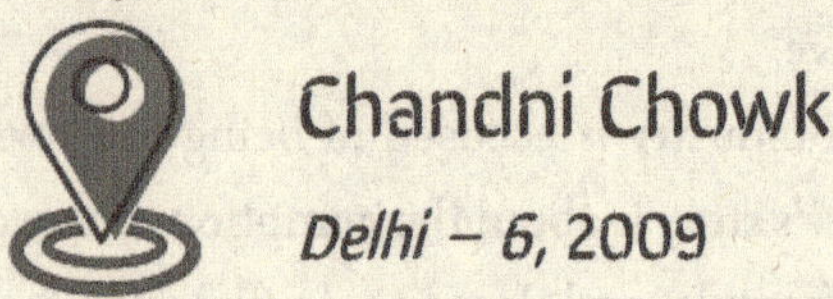

Chandni Chowk

Delhi – 6, 2009

Tujhse milna purani Dilli mein, chhod aaye nishani Dilli mein,
Ballimaran se Daribe talak, teri meri kahaani Dilli mein.

Gulzar recounted a love story in the lanes of Old Delhi – an area evocatively called the Moonlight Square – through a hit song in *Bunty Aur Babli*. Chandni Chowk has many historical and literary antecedents, but they never hit the silver screen. Even Gulzar's television series *Mirza Ghalib* wasn't shot on location – rather, it was made in a Bombay studio.

That changed when two Delhi boys released film sets (for the large part) in Chandni Chowk. Akshay Kumar wasn't born in Delhi, but grew up in Chandni Chowk, and played a cook in a roadside paratha stall in (the early parts of) *Chandni Chowk to China*. The longer and more passionate ode came in the form of Rakeysh Omprakash Mehra's *Delhi – 6* – a film that captured the innards of the capital city really well (despite being shot in a Rajasthani small town, where the lanes were recreated and landmarks like the Jama Masjid added digitally to the frames).

Bollywood's forays into Delhi until then had largely been on the main thoroughfares – India Gate was very much in the limelight, as were the shiny promenades of central Delhi. Qutab Minar was always the easiest shorthand for the city, and the Metro (running past a gigantic statue of Hanuman) became the symbol of Delhi in the mid-2000s. *Delhi – 6* referred to the postal code of Chandni Chowk, and was probably the most intricate canvas on which a movie has been set.[8] The maze of lanes and bylanes, the homes and shops set cheek by jowl, the purveyors of delicious snacks, the casual racism, and the religious festivities that ran round-the-year and round-the-clock were all presented without sugar-coating or romanticizing them. An NRI's sense of

8. This was by no means the first attempt to showcase Chandni Chowk. B.R. Chopra directed *Chandni Chowk*, a love story set only partially in the eponymous location. The film became a hit and allowed him to start his own company, B.R. Films. (The hero of the film goes off to Egypt, thus making a case for calling it *Chandni Chowk to Cairo*!)

wonder at the place's history was juxtaposed against a resident's urge to break free of its shackles – both perfectly identifiable emotions in the older parts of Delhi.

While *Delhi – 6* didn't do very well commercially and critically, it was at the forefront of a trend of showcasing the 'real' Delhi in Bollywood. Later that year, Anurag Kashyap's *Dev D* explored Paharganj, a grungier part of town known for youngsters tripping in its psychedelic cafes and lodges. Maneesh Sharma's *Band Baaja Baaraat* was set in another non-glamorous part – Paschim Vihar – and captured the entrepreneurial spirit of Delhi perfectly. What *BBB* started with the college culture, *Rockstar* completed by bringing in the inter-college rivalries of Delhi University. Over the last decade, Hindi films have dug deep into Delhi's colonies, even branching out into the adjoining cities of the NCR, and finding the crazies, the romantics, the do-gooders and the go-getters the city is famous for. As the song went

Yeh Dilli hai mere yaar, bas ishq mohabbat pyaar.
Basti hai mastano ki Dilli, gali hai deewano ki Dilli six!

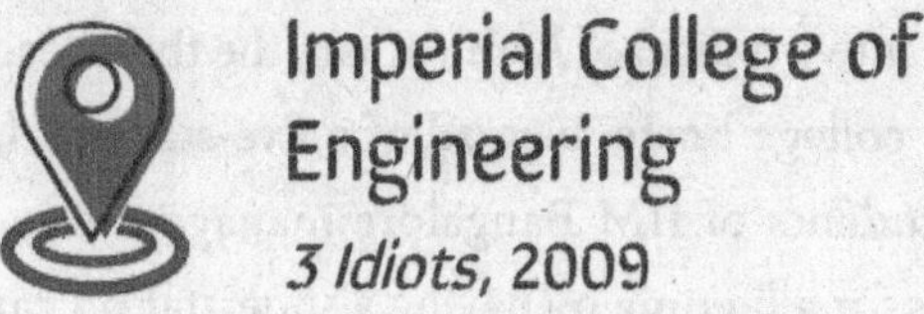

Imperial College of Engineering

3 Idiots, 2009

If *Taare Zameen Par*'s Ishaan Awasthi hadn't met the inspirational teacher who would unlock his talent, what would he have become? He would have most likely become a middle-class lemming, who sacrifices his talent at the altar of an assured career – engineering. In other words, he would have become *3 Idiots*'s Farhan Qureshi. But then again, Farhan too met an inspirational teacher – at the Imperial College of Engineering.

Rajkumar Hirani and his co-writer Abhijat Joshi have a penchant for the 'Imperial' epithet to denote institutions of academic excellence. After the Imperial College of Medicine in *Munna Bhai MBBS,* they decided to name the IIT (Indian Institute of Technology) clone of *3 Idiots* similarly. Imperial

College of Engineering was set in the campus of Indian Institute of Management (IIM), Bangalore – finalized after the production team looked at some 400 colleges all over India. And in a 'method' move typical of Aamir Khan, the three lead actors stayed at the college hostel instead of a five-star hotel, which meant the students of IIM Bangalore managed to get after-dinner stories for a lifetime by having a superstar on campus.[9]

The original source material – Chetan Bhagat's *Five Point Someone: What Not to Do at IIT* – was clearly set in IIT Delhi, while the film created a fictitious but easily identifiable college. Led by the formidable Viru 'Virus' Sahasrabuddhe (Boman Irani), Imperial College of Engineering embodied the best and worst of India's 'engineering' gold rush – where millions of bright youngsters enter a rat race to get a shot at the lucrative jobs that lie at the end of a B.Tech degree. Not an ailing parent, not even a student's suicide, is enough to modify the college's modus operandi. The character of Rancho (Aamir Khan) becomes the conscience of the college, where he repeatedly demonstrates the futility of mindless education – inspiring his classmates

9. Hostels, classrooms, canteens and other places on the IIM Bangalore campus were immortalized on screen – including Lincoln Square where the all-important batch photograph of *3 Idiots* is taken. And why is it called Lincoln? Probably because it's located in between Blocks A, B and E.

towards excellence, not success. His carefree genius is directly at odds with the Imperial College of Engineering's hard-nosed, studious attempts at success. And it eventually ends with his victory on the banks of a pristine blue lake in Ladakh, symbolic in its beauty when compared to the rough stony architecture of the management institute that passed off as the country's top engineering college.

Ever since the IITs became the gold-standard of Indian education, they also triggered a mad rush to join them – often at considerable loss to the students' self-esteem and general life skills. *3 Idiots* showcased just this, becoming one of India's most successful films of all times, striking a chord with both students and parents. With a more confident young generation and the emergence of other careers, engineering study in India is on a decline. Between 2014 and 2020, the number of IIT aspirants have dropped by nearly 40 per cent. While the economics of demand and supply is probably the prime mover behind this, one wonders if the cold-blooded stodginess of Imperial College of Engineering had an impact on this trend.

Tomfoolery on the campus of IIM Bangalore, one of India's top B-schools masquerading as one of India's E-schools.

Image courtesy of Vinod Chopra Films

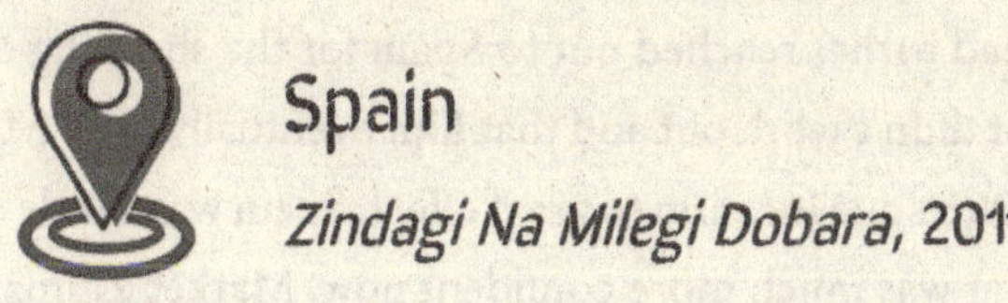

Spain

Zindagi Na Milegi Dobara, 2011

In July 2010, Madrid saw an unusual Indian tourist. Director Anurag Kashyap had received multiple versions of scripts written around gang wars in a small town in Jharkhand. He went to Madrid with all the versions, locked himself up in a hotel room for four days and produced a workable script of the films that would eventually become *Gangs of Wasseypur*. The reason he chose Spain was because his then-girlfriend, Kalki Koechlin, was shooting for *Zindagi Na Milegi Dobara* there and, thus, became the first Indian tourist who went to Spain because of the film.

The script of *Zindagi Na Milegi Dobara* – written by Zoya Akhtar and Reema Kagti – had three friends going on an extended bachelor's trip in Spain. Once the script was locked, the producers – Excel Entertainment – got in touch with Turespaña, the Spanish tourism authority, to figure out a co-promotion deal. Excel had earlier reached out to Spain for the shooting of *Don*, but that didn't work out and that film eventually used Malaysia as a picturesque location to great effect. Spain was a little unsure then, but was much more confident now. Market estimates say the tourism board put in the equivalent of 500,000 Euros to promote the film, and contributed significant on-ground support to various aspects of film-making. Apart from the monetary value, the Spanish authorities stepped in to make the permission process smooth for all the locations, which included tough ones like the Bull Run and La Tomatina.

Barcelona. Costa Brava. Buñol. Seville. Pamplona. Each place the trio went to had a unique feel and the leads had an exciting activity to complete. The trip was designed to showcase the best of Spain in terms of tourism activities, with inputs from Turespaña. The inclusion of flamenco dancing – with the song '*Senorita*' – was suggested by the tourism authority itself! Marketing experts have said that *Zindagi Na Milegi Dobara* was the first attempt to create a travel brochure in the form of cinema, and it succeeded. The film is now a case study in a marketing course in Spain!

And, of course, the tourist numbers from India zoomed. There was a 100 per cent spike in visa applications in July 2011 alone – the month the film released. And the craze had started even before the release, when the trailers were shown. Nearly 1,15,000 Indian tourists visited Spain in 2011 – up more than 50 per cent from the previous year. An avalanche had started with individual tourists, office groups and bachelor parties going on curated tours to the film's locations, culminating in the IIFA Awards being held at Madrid in 2016. Spain was suddenly the new Switzerland.

And one more thing… enrolment into flamenco dance classes also shot up!

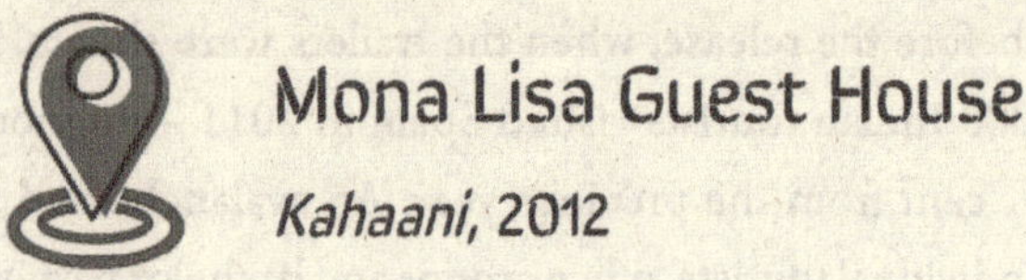

Mona Lisa Guest House

Kahaani, 2012

In February 2012, when Sujoy Ghosh's *Kahaani* started its successful run at Kolkata's Menoka Cinema (among other places), audiences did the obvious thing after watching the film. They walked across to Sarat Bose Road – not even a kilometre from the cinema hall – to see Mona Lisa Guest House, a nondescript (zero star, as per the film) lodge that achieved an iconic status with the popularity of the film.

Kahaani, which came three months after *The Dirty Picture*, made a superstar out of Vidya Balan... and Kolkata. It was probably the first film to be set in Kolkata that didn't show Victoria Memorial or the Howrah Bridge, old or new. Sujoy Ghosh – coming off two flops, *Home Delivery* and *Aladin* – had major trouble securing financing for his film 'because, on paper, a pregnant woman screaming for her missing husband on the streets of Kolkata doesn't make sense'.

But Ghosh stuck to his guns. He says, 'I enjoy setting my films in Kolkata ... like Woody Allen does almost everything in New York City.' He knew the city really well, the place he grew up in and where his father drove a taxi for a living. Thus, this city, with its distinctive old-world charm, became the setting for a thriller in which the protagonist was visiting the place for the first time. The newcomer's gaze helped a pan-India audience soak in the minutiae, the people and the atmosphere of the city more effectively.

During the Durga Puja of 2010, Ghosh and his crew booked Mona Lisa Guest House for 10 days paying a princely sum of ₹40,000. The timing was critical to the film, as was the location of the guest house. Ghosh got the geography spot on and – as shown in the movie – the actual guest house is also about a couple of kilometres from the Kalighat Police Station, where Vidya Balan's character – Vidya Bagchi – makes her first port of call in the search for her husband. Other locations – Camac Street, Mocambo restaurant, Thakurpukur, Kumartuli – also appeared in the script as per their real distances from each other. Triangular Park, where the climax unfolds, is also within walking distance from the guest house. The slightly rundown look of the guest house, complete with its tattered guest register, fitted in with the story. Its promise of 'running hot water' in the form of a little attendant was a nod towards a Satyajit Ray film, which had a similar sequence. Room number 15 on the top floor, where Vidya Bagchi stayed, is an actual room – a 20x14–feet suite offering a great view of the road it is located on.

As soon as the film released, Mona Lisa Guest House saw a sharp rise in both casual visitors as well as fans who came from outside Calcutta to stay in room number 15 for a night and watch the film at a nearby theatre. From being just another lodge, Mona Lisa is now a tourist attraction and a landmark in the city. *Ek minit*, that's not all. In a quirky coincidence, there's a hair and skin parlour located on a parallel lane. It's called Bob!

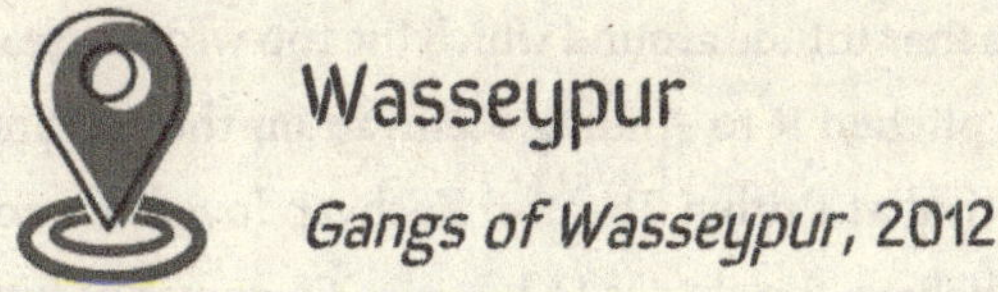

Wasseypur

Gangs of Wasseypur, 2012

Mumbai's Versova is a haven for film industry hopefuls. One evening in 2009, three such strugglers – Zeishan Quadri, Sachin Ladia and Akhilesh Jaiswal – watched the classic Brazilian crime drama, *City of God,* to educate Zeishan, the relative newcomer in the trio, about good cinema. Zeishan was unimpressed. He dismissed the story, saying it was no match for the goings-on of his hometown. Or more accurately, the mohalla of Dhanbad he was from – Wasseypur.

Wasseypur, named after the brother – Wassey Mian – of a local zamindar was formed in 1964, but isn't found on any official map of Dhanbad. Instead, it resides deep in the minds of its residents as an area of narrow lanes and bylanes, where shootouts abound and gangs proliferate. It is a place where your worth isn't measured by the size of your bank balance, but by the size of your balls.

This was the attitude around which the trio wrote a treatment. They then pitched it to Anurag Kashyap on the sidelines of a theatre festival at Prithvi Theatre. Kashyap loved the concept, but didn't believe the stories to be true. To convince him, they came back later with Zeishan and newspaper clippings of the various incidents.

The stories were as fantastic as they were detailed. In December 2004, shooters belonging to the Sabir Alam gang, led by one Sultan, attacked the home of Fahim Khan, a rival gangster. The neat detail about the attack's timing was that it happened during an episode of *Kyunki Saas Bhi Kabhi Bahu Thi*, which kept the streets deserted and the target indoors. The attack happened a couple of lanes away from Zeishan's home, and he came back home in 2009 to research the real incidents, to bring authenticity to his explosive stories.

Gangs of Wasseypur was based on the real-life rivalry of Fahim Khan (who became Faizal Khan in the film, played by Nawazuddin Siddiqui) and Sabir Alam (who became Shamsad Alam, played by Rajkummar Rao), studded with memorable characters like Sultan Qureshi, Ramadhir Singh, Durga,

Mohsina, Perpendicular and Definite (the last one played by Zeishan himself). From the novel-like research initially given to him, Anurag Kashyap crafted the script as a crime saga, tracing the history of mafia in the coal-belt of Dhanbad and adjoining West Bengal. Starting from the 1940s with the tale of the legendary Sultana Daku, it came down to the early 2000s – covering three generations of the Khan family and their enmities with other gangsters, politicians and their own relatives.

Gangs of Wasseypur was a path-breaking effort in both form and content. The saga of 70 years was told over nearly six hours, split between two films that released a few weeks apart. The films soon got a cult following, created an international market for 'indie' films, and strengthened curiosity about the small towns of India. And it all happened because of the mohalla of Wasseypur about which insiders said, '*Ek hi jaan hai. Ya toh* Allah *lega, ya mohalla.*'

The poster of *Gangs of Wasseypur* dropped enough hints about its characters, its period, and its milieu to set the film on its way to becoming a cult classic.

Image copyright: Viacom 18 Studios

China

Dangal, 2016

Little Lolita's Monkey God Uncle. Let's Wrestle, Dad. The Teacher with the Hiccups.

Mandarin Chinese uses what is called 'ideograms', with most of its characters (letters) being a visual representation of the ideas they represent. Once you know that, it is easy to figure out what these phrases mean. These are the Chinese titles of Hindi films released in the world's second-largest movie market. *Bajrangi Bhaijaan*, *Dangal* and *Hichki* – with their evocative new titles – made tons of money in the new Holy Grail of Hindi cinema.

The story of Hindi cinema in China started with *Dangal*, but the prequel was Rajkumar Hirani's *3 Idiots*. The 2009 film didn't actually release in China – it garnered massive popularity through pirated DVDs, reaching the top 20 of Douban's (China's top movie reviews site) list of all-time great movies, rubbing shoulders with the likes of *Interstellar, Inception* and *Wall-E.*

Given the limit on the number of international films that can be imported and exhibited in China, the next Aamir Khan film to be marketed widely and given a nationwide release was *PK*. By this time, Aamir Khan had an active fan club in China, and he went on a multi-city tour to tremendous adulation. The critique on organized religion went on to become the first Indian film to cross the 100 million Yuan mark. Aamir's next two films – *Dangal* and *Secret Superstar* – were such monster hits that they overtook Marvel/Disney global franchises in the box-office stakes. People were doing flash mobs and tribute videos, basically going crazy over Mi-Shu (Mi being the short form of 'Aamir' and Shu being the short form of Shu-hu, or Uncle). *Dangal* had a planned marketing strategy to first show the film to Chinese film industry influencers, who recommended the film effusively and kicked off its record-breaking run. Even with Aamir Khan in a guest role, *Secret Superstar* upstaged *Black Panther* at the box-office, and paved the way for two unlikely successes – *Hindi Medium* and *Hichki*. Both films were moderate hits in India, but made many times their Indian revenue in China.

China also has a hyper-competitive education system like India. Hence, tales of a maverick rebelling against the system seem to find an instant connect there. Sometimes the adversary is the education system directly (*3 Idiots, Hindi Medium, Hichki*). In some cases, it is the religious or social system (*PK, Secret Superstar*), or even the system of a national identity (*Bajrangi Bhaijaan*). China has taken to Indian emotional stories – mainstays of classic Bollywood – in a big way, rejecting big-budget extravaganzas like *Thugs of Hindostan* or even *Baahubali 2*, neither of which managed a fraction of how much *Dangal* made. Meanwhile, when Chinese premier, Xi Jinping, met his Indian counterpart, Narendra Modi, he effusively praised *Dangal* and asked for more films like that. Over the last few years, China and India have faced off several times on trade and politics, and yet, Bollywood has gone from strength to strength in Chinese cinemas. Mi-Shu's soft power, FTW!

Toilet

Toilet: Ek Prem Katha, 2017

On 12 June 2017, Prime Minister Narendra Modi tweeted, 'Good effort to further the message of cleanliness. 125 crore Indians have to continue working together to create a Swachh Bharat.' This could have been a regular tweet about his pet project – Swachh Bharat Abhiyan – except he was reacting to the trailer of a Hindi film. The movie – produced by and starring Akshay Kumar – was planned as a public outreach support to the prime minister's mission. The star had met PM Modi earlier and had tweeted, 'Met PM @ narendramodi and got the opportunity to tell him about my upcoming *Toilet: Ek Prem Katha*. His smile at just the title made my day.'

Akshay Kumar had a series of hit comedies in the 2000s, which was a significant shift from his action hero image since his debut. From 2014 onwards, he found a niche in patriotic, action thrillers (*Holiday, Baby, Airlift, Naam Shabana*), playing no-nonsense operatives saving his country from harm. With *Toilet: Ek Prem Katha*, he found a micro-niche of raising women's issues based on real events. After *Toilet*, he made *Pad Man* (based on the life of Arunachalam Muruganantham, inventor of a low-cost sanitary napkin) and *Mission Mangal* (based on India's women-led Mars Mission).

Toilet: Ek Prem Katha was based on the inspiring story of Shivram and Anita Narre, a couple who built a toilet to save themselves from the unhygienic and unsafe practice of open defecation. That there were several other claims to the original story indicate that people across the country have fought their own personal battles for hygiene, and *Toilet* ended up being their collective story on screen.

Governments – state or Centre – have often funded films with positive social messages, though they often end up being specialized vehicles. Bollywood picking up a project on a prime minister's request is relatively rare. Manoj Kumar making *Upkar* on Lal Bahadur Shastri's request was probably the only other movie made on such an explicit request. Till *Toilet* came along and became a massive hit, also becoming Akshay Kumar's highest-grossing film. While some critics felt the film endorsed the Swachh Bharat Abhiyan a bit too stridently, a popular film with a positive message does have a strong grass-root impact. According to Parameswaran Iyer, secretary at the ministry of drinking water and sanitation, 'I realized we needed some disruption in the ministry... We had PM Modi, our communicator-in-chief, and then we had Akshay with his movie *Toilet*, which was transformational.'

With strong government and public support, Akshay Kumar is well on his way to become something of a Manoj Kumar redux. His announced films are mostly based on socio-patriotic themes. Including one familiar topic. At the launch of a book about the Swachh Bharat Mission, the UNICEF (United Nations International Children's Emergency Fund) representative in India revealed that women have taken on the role of constructing toilets. In 2018, about 2,000 women in Jharkhand's Simdega district managed to build 7,000 toilets in just five days. Reacting to this, Akshay Kumar said, '[You have] given me the plot for *Toilet: Ek Prem Katha 2*.'

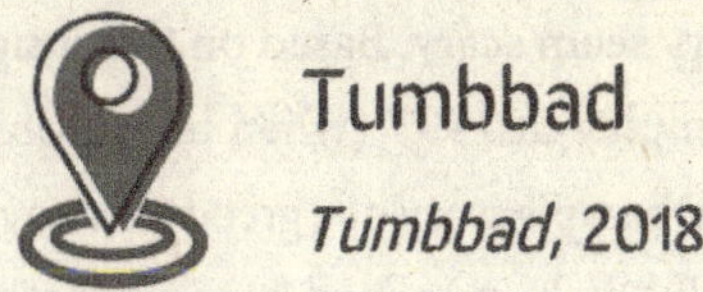

Tumbbad

Tumbbad, 2018

The movie tells us that because of a curse by the gods, it always rains in the village of Tumbbad. This meant that a major part of the film could only be shot during the months of July and August – the rainy season. The shooting was spread over three monsoons, when the cinematographer got his overcast days and rains, or rain machines were used if the actual rain was not enough. The journey of *Tumbbad*, a folk horror tale, took two decades to finish, from concept to release, and the landscape played the biggest role of all.

Tumbbad is that rarest of rare Hindi film that thrives purely on atmosphere. Director Rahi Anil Barve first heard the Marathi story – on which the film is based – from a friend at the Nagzira wildlife sanctuary. That night, he was scared out of his wits. When he read the story later, he found it to be quite unremarkable. It was his friend's narration and the spooky atmosphere of the jungle that made the story seem scary. Based on this insight, he started writing the screenplay in 1997 (when he was just 18). Marathi writer Narayan Dharap's story of a greedy moneylender was what Barve heard. With it, he punched in another story of a grandmother possessed by demons – by the same writer. Years after he wrote the first draft of the story, he began shooting in 2008 with Nawazuddin Siddiqui. However, the project had to be abandoned because the producer backed out. Shooting started again in 2012 with producers Sohum Shah (who also acted in the lead role) and Anand Gandhi. When Barve and Shah saw the edited version, it didn't quite match with their vision of the film. In a daring act, they rewrote and reshot the entire movie till the final product was truly genre-defining.

The 'bible' of *Tumbbad* was a 700-page storyboard created by Barve. A trained illustrator, he created the striking frames in an exceptionally detailed exercise that the cinematographer (Pankaj Kumar) and production designers (Nitin Zihani Choudhary and Rakesh Yadav) strove to match. The story of a man's greed to steal gold from the womb of a goddess, protected by a fallen god, Hastar, has shades of several cautionary mythological fables. The story was set between 1918 and 1947, and the action moved between contrasting colour palettes. From a 1930s restored bus on the open plains of Konkan Maharashtra (framed in blue and cold grey) to shadowy action in the deep, dark well-like womb (which had splashes of gold on blood red). Since it was a period film, the entire lighting set-up comprised only of 50 lanterns and lamps. The eerie, atmospheric music was composed by Jesper Kyd – who composes music for video games (like *Assassin's Creed* and *Hitman*), and whose only reference of Hindi film music was *Ram Lakhan* (given to him by co-director Adesh Prasad)!

Tumbbad is the name of a real village in Maharashtra, where – as legends go – untold riches are hidden. *Tumbbad* builds on such legends and creates almost a parallel universe. This universe looks exactly like the one we inhabit, but moves ominously to provide us with a cautionary tale. Which we then ignore at our own peril!

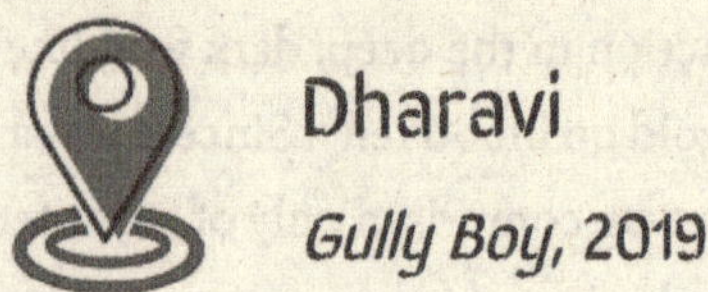

Dharavi

Gully Boy, 2019

'Paida hua pala badha hateli ilake mein,
Yahan sabko karne di pateli har naake pe,
Sabse hatkar sabse kattar, mooh khola toh sar par fattar,
Sabse khattar-naak Bombay *sattar.'*

Zoya Akhtar listened to these lyrics while shooting *Dil Dhadakne Do*, and was intrigued enough to first find out about the performer – Naved Shaikh (aka Naezy) – and then make a film on him and another Mumbai rapper, Vivian Fernandes (aka Divine), with whom Naezy often partnered.

The '*Bombay sattar*' referred to the pin code 400070 of Kurla, where Naezy lived, and as the script got written, that got changed to '*Bombay satrah*' (400017) – the pin code of Dharavi, one of Asia's largest slums, which packs in more than 7,00,000 people in just over 2 square kilometres. Zoya Akhtar later called shooting in Dharavi as the 'best shooting experience [she has] had in this country' as the people there are helpful without being starstruck because so many foreign films have been shot there.

Production designer of *Gully Boy*, Suzanne Caplan Merwanji, said, 'Dharavi is a character in itself in the film', and indeed, much of Murad's (Ranveer Singh) struggles and inspirations come from the claustrophobic surroundings of the slum. *Gully Boy* is probably the only mainstream Hindi film that was located almost entirely in a real slum and not within sanitized sets. A parking lot in the middle of Dharavi was used to build the set of a slum within the slum. The set had 130 houses and 12 shops, including Murad's house and the lanes just outside it. The cramped reality of Murad counterpointed brilliantly with the expanse of his ambitions. One memorable scene in the movie showed Murad measuring out the bathroom in Sky's (Kalki Koechlin) flat with his feet, and finding it bigger than his entire home.

The atmosphere of Dharavi was not only in the sets but also in the lines. Zoya Akhtar and co-writer Reema Kagti wrote the screenplay in English, and dialogue writer Vijay Maurya converted it into the realistic street-lingo of regular Mumbaikars with inputs from 20-something rappers, who helped him get the lingo just right. Without resorting to the usual clichés of Mumbai *tapori* lingo, Maurya churned out lines that were both real and catchy. '*Boht* hard' as a compliment for sharp poetry (or anything good, in general) quickly became a cult favourite.

And the final element of the Dharavi jigsaw was the characters – especially Ranveer Singh in the lead role. After a larger-than-life Alauddin Khilji, Singh lost weight and effected a miraculous transformation as a nearly invisible Muslim youth, who came alive only when he was pouring his anger out on paper and on stage. The supporting cast – Vijay Raaz, Amruta Subhash and Vijay Verma – were as real, exuding both the grime and the energy of Dharavi.

Gully Boy is that inspiring story of every talented artiste breaking through his shackles ('*Yeh shabdon ka jwala bediyan pighlayega*'). It is also the story of a Dharavi resident, proudly making his origins a part of his creative output ('*Kidhar ho, kidhar ho tum abhi? Bombay satrah mein, bhai!*').

Bibliography

Abbasi, Yasir. *Yeh Un Dinoñ Ki Baat Hai: Urdu Memoirs of Cinema Legends*. New Delhi: Bloomsbury, 2018.

Ahmed, Rauf. *Shammi Kapoor: The Game Changer*. Noida: Om Books International, 2016.

Baradwaj, Rangan and Man⌧iratn⌧am. *Conversations with Mani Ratnam*. New Delhi: Penguin, 2013.

Bhatia, Sidharth. *Cinema Modern: The Navketan Story*. Noida: Harper Collins Publishers India, 2011.

Chopra, Anupama. *Sholay: The Making of a Classic*. New Delhi: Penguin, 2000.

Dasgupta, Shamya. *Don't Disturb the Dead: The Story of the Ramsay Brothers*. Noida: Harper Collins Publishers India, 2017.

Desai, Meghnad. *Pakeezah: An Ode to a Bygone World*. Noida: Harper Collins Publishers India, 2013.

Dwyer, Rachel. *Yash Chopra: Fifty Years in Indian Cinema*. New Delhi: Roli Books, 2002.

Kothari, Jigna, and Supriya Madangarli. *Gangs of Wasseypur: The Making of a Modern Classic.* Noida: Harper Collins Publishers India, 2013.

Manwani, Akshay. *Sahir Ludhianvi: The People's Poet.* Noida: Harper Collins Publishers India, 2013.

Mehra, Rakeysh Omprakash, Kamlesh Pandey, and Rensil D'Silva. *Rang De Basanti: The Shooting Script.* Noida: Om Books International, 2014.

Mehta, Vinod. *Meena Kumari: The Classic Biography.* Noida: Harper Collins Publishers India, 2013.

Mukherjee, Debashree. *Bombay Hustle: Making Movies in a Colonial City.* New York: Columbia University Press, 2020.

Nanda, Ritu. *Raj Kapoor: Speaks.* New Delhi: Penguin.

Paadhye, Anitaa. *Goldie: The Man and His Movies.* New Delhi: Amaryllis, 2020.

Puri, Kamlesh. *My Father, the Villain: The Life and Times of Madan Puri.* New Delhi: Bloomsbury, 2016.

Roy, Arundhati. *In Which Annie Gives It Those Ones: The Original Screenplay.* New Delhi: Penguin, 2003.

Sathya Saran. *Ten Years with Guru Dutt: Abrar Alvi's Journey.* Gurgaon: Penguin Random House, 2020.

Usman, Yasser. *Guru Dutt: An Unfinished Story.* New Delhi: Simon & Schuster, 2020.

Zankar, Anil. *Mughal-e-Azam: Legend as Epic.* Noida: Harper Collins Publishers India, 2013.

Acknowledgements

Abhishek Dubey, Ajit Andhare, Akhil Jain and Amit Ramsay for their help with sourcing the images.

Subrat Mohanty for sharing his voluminous insights about cinema.

Thomas Abraham, Poulomi Chatterjee, Swarnima Narayan and Ansila Thomas of Hachette India, for indulging me at every turn and turning my ramblings into a dream series.

Echo Chamber, Sobuj Sangho, Kwiz Group, for fuelling many trivial pursuits.

Rita Chaudhuri, Shivaramakrishnan K and Nilendu Misra, for always being ready to talk movies.

Trishna, Dyujoy and Drishti Chaudhuri, for always being there.

Acknowledgement